BEADS OF LIFE

Eastern and Southern African Beadwork from Canadian Collections

Marie-Louise Labelle

MERCURY SERIES
CULTURAL STUDIES PAPER 78
CANADIAN MUSEUM OF CIVILIZATION

© 2005 Canadian Museum of Civilization Corporation

Published by the
Canadian Museum of Civilization Corporation (CMCC)
100 Laurier Street
P.O. Box 3100, Station B
Gatineau, Quebec J8X 4H2

PRINTED IN CANADA

Manager, Publishing: Deborah Brownrigg
Editor: Ursula Desmarteau for Aubut and Associates
Mercury Series Design: Hangar 13
Printer: Custom Printers, Renfrew, Ontario

Front cover photograph: Bag (detail); San, Botswana; Textile Museum of Canada, Toronto T86.0105; Photo: © Canadian Museum of Civilization, Steven Darby

Back cover photographs:
Top: Doll; Tsonga, South Africa
Middle: Necklaces; Maasai, Kenya
Bottom: Necklace; Zulu, South Africa

Library and Archives Canada Cataloguing in Publication

Labelle, Marie-Louise

Beads of life : Eastern and Southern African beadwork from Canadian collections

(Mercury series, ISSN 0361-1854)

(Cultural Studies Paper, ISSN 1707-8970 ; 78)

Includes an abstract in French.
Includes bibliographical references.
ISBN 0-660-19402-3
Cat. no. NM23-2/78E

1. Beadwork – Africa, East – Exhibitions.
2. Beadwork – Africa, Southern – Exhibitions.
3. Africa, East – Social life and customs – Exhibitions.
4. Africa, Southern – Social life and custom – Exhibitions.
5. Clothing and dress – Africa, East – Exhibitions.
6. Clothing and dress – Africa, Southern – Exhibitions.
I. Canadian Museum of Civilization.
II. Title.
III. Series.
IV. Series: Cultural studies paper (Canadian Museum of Civilization) ; no. 78.

NK3650.A353G34 2005   746'.09676   C2004-980349-2

Object of the Mercury Series

This series is designed to permit the rapid dissemination of information pertaining to the disciplines in which the Canadian Museum of Civilization Corporation is active. Considered an important reference by the scientific community, the Mercury Series comprises over 400 specialized publications on Canada's history and prehistory. Due to its specialized audience, the series consists largely of monographs published in the language of the author. In the interest of making information available quickly, normal production procedures have been abbreviated. As a result, grammatical and typographical errors may occur. Your indulgence is requested.

But de la collection Mercure

La collection Mercure vise à diffuser rapidement le résultat de travaux dans les disciplines qui relèvent des sphères d'activités du Musée canadien des civilisations. Considérée comme un apport important dans la communauté scientifique, la collection Mercure présente plus de 400 publications spécialisées portant sur l'héritage canadien préhistorique et historique. Comme la collection s'adresse à un public spécialisé, celle-ci est constituée essentiellement de monographies publiées dans la langue des auteurs. Pour assurer la prompte distribution des exemplaires imprimés, les étapes de l'édition ont été abrégées. En conséquence, certaines coquilles ou fautes de grammaire peuvent subsister : c'est pour-quoi nous réclamons votre indulgence.

How to Obtain Mercury Series Titles

E-mail: publications@civilization.ca
Web: cyberboutique.civilization.ca
Telephone: 1 819 776-8387 or, toll-free
             1 800 555-5621 (North America)
Mail: Mail Order Services
             Canadian Museum of Civilization
             100 Laurier Street
             P.O. Box 3100, Station B
             Gatineau, Quebec J8X 4H2

Comment se procurer les titres parus dans la collection Mercure

Courriel :   publications@civilisations.ca
Web :   cyberboutique.civilisations.ca
Téléphone :   1 819 776-8387 ou sans frais,
              en Amérique du Nord seulement,
              1 800 555-5621
Poste :   Service des commandes postales
              Musée canadien des civilisations
              100, rue Laurier
              C.P. 3100, succursale B
              Gatineau (Québec) J8X 4H2

For Carmelle Bégin

ABSTRACT

This work is an introduction to the beadwork of eastern and southern Africa based on an analysis of pieces from collections in Canadian museums and universities. It accompanies the exhibition **Beads of Life: Eastern and Southern African Adornments** which opened at the Canadian Museum of Civilization (CMC) on April 14, 2005.

For several years now, beadwork has been growing in popularity. Perpetuating long-established traditions, the women of eastern and southern Africa continue to make beaded ornaments today, but in forms that are changing constantly, and under circumstances that are radically different from those of earlier times. Although the functions and meanings of today's African beadwork have become increasingly difficult to define, this book attempts to provide a basis for understanding the origins of this art.

The author begins by examining the materials that were used for clothing and ornaments prior to the arrival of glass beads, and clarifies their functions in relation to protection and to the identification of status. When imported beads arrived in massive quantities, they continued to fulfill these same functions for a time. The author examines some of the aesthetic rules based on the use of three essential colours, white, red and blue, and describes how the combination of these three contrasting colours often rested upon socio-religious principles. The book also describes the principal items of clothing and adornment that were worn to indicate an individual's status within a society, and concludes with an examination of the contemporary aspects of beadwork and its continuity with tradition, especially as viewed by Canadians from eastern and southern Africa who were consulted for the exhibition.

Marie-Louise Labelle is the curator of **Beads of Life: Eastern and Southern African Adornments** at the Canadian Museum of Civilization. She undertook extensive fieldwork among the Maasai and Samburu of Kenya during the 1980s, and has a Ph.D. in Social Anthropology from the *Centre d'études africaines* of the *École des Hautes Études en Sciences Sociales* in Paris.

RÉSUMÉ

Cet ouvrage est une introduction au perlage d'Afrique orientale et australe, basé sur l'analyse de pièces provenant des collections des universités et musées canadiens. Il accompagne l'exposition **Perles de vie – Parures de l'Afrique orientale et australe**, qui a ouvert ses portes au Musée canadien des civilisations (MCC) le 14 avril 2005.

Depuis quelques années, le perlage connaît une popularité grandissante. Les femmes d'Afrique de l'Est et du Sud, suivant une longue tradition, continuent aujourd'hui à fabriquer des ornements perlés, mais sous des formes en constante mutation et dans des circonstances radicalement différentes d'autrefois. Alors que les fonctions et significations du perlage actuel semblent de plus en plus difficiles à cerner, cet ouvrage tente de faire le point en remontant aux origines de cet art.

L'auteur examine tout d'abord les matériaux qui, avant l'arrivée des perles de pâte de verre, étaient autrefois utilisés pour la parure et les vêtements, afin de dégager leurs fonctions de protection et d'identification du statut. Lorsque les perles d'importation sont arrivées en masse, elles ont continué à remplir, pour un temps, ces fonctions. L'auteur tente de dégager quelques règles esthétiques basées sur l'utilisation de trois couleurs essentielles, le blanc, le rouge et le bleu. Selon elle, la combinaison de ces trois couleurs contrastées pourrait reposer sur des principes socio-religieux. Enfin elle énumère les principaux ornements et vêtements qui indiquent le statut des personnes dans la société, avant d'examiner les aspects contemporains du perlage et leur continuité avec la tradition, notamment à l'aide de réflexions des membres de la communauté canadienne originaires d'Afrique de l'Est et du Sud, consultés pour l'exposition.

Marie-Louise Labelle est la conservatrice de l'exposition **Perles de vie – Parures de l'Afrique orientale et australe** au Musée canadien des civilisations. Elle a effectué des recherches parmi les Maasaï et les Samburu du Kenya dans les années 80, et détient un doctorat en Anthropologie sociale du Centre d'études africaines de l'École des Hautes Études en Sciences Sociales à Paris.

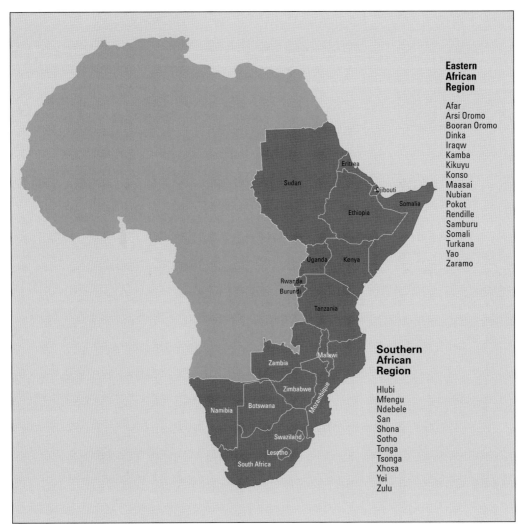

Eastern African Region

Afar
Arsi Oromo
Booran Oromo
Dinka
Iraqw
Kamba
Kikuyu
Konso
Maasai
Nubian
Pokot
Rendille
Samburu
Somali
Turkana
Yao
Zaramo

Southern African Region

Hlubi
Mfengu
Ndebele
San
Shona
Sotho
Tonga
Tsonga
Xhosa
Yei
Zulu

Eritrea
Sudan
Djibouti
Somalia
Ethiopia
Uganda
Kenya
Rwanda
Burundi
Tanzania
Zambia
Malawi
Zimbabwe
Mozambique
Namibia
Botswana
Swaziland
Lesotho
South Africa

Countries of Eastern and Southern Africa and list of cultural groups.

CONTENTS

Abstract vi

Résumé vii

Map of Africa viii

Acknowledgements xi

Introduction 1

**Chapter 1: Eastern and Southern African Beadwork from
Canadian Collections** 5

Chapter 2: Materials of Early Ornament and Clothing 15

Chapter 3: Glass Beads and Colour Interpretation 49

Chapter 4: Aesthetic Principles of Beadwork 63

Chapter 5: Status Clothing and Ornaments 107

Chapter 6: Beads of Life 153

Conclusion 177

Selected Bibliography 179

ACKNOWLEDGEMENTS

I would like to thank staff at the many Canadian museums and universities who allowed me access to their collections and lent artifacts to the **Beads of Life** exhibition. These include the Textile Museum of Canada, the Redpath Museum, the Royal Ontario Museum, the Vancouver Museum, the Museum of Anthropology at the University of British Columbia, the Provincial Museum of Alberta, the Glenbow Museum, the Manitoba Museum, the New Brunswick Museum, the Kelowna Museum, the Anthropology Department of the Université de Montréal, the Department of Museums and Collections Services of the University of Alberta and the Anthropology Museum at the University of Winnipeg. I am also grateful to all the individuals who lent items from their private collections.

I am deeply indebted to the many Canadians of eastern and southern African origin who shared their life stories with me, while also providing important information and a unique perspective on the objects presented in **Beads of Life**.

I wish to thank all the staff at the Canadian Museum of Civilization who participated in the exhibition project and the publication. I am especially grateful to Sylvie Laflamme, Head of Inter-Library Loans, Conservator Caroline Marchand who initiated me into the intricacies of beadwork techniques, Deborah Brownrigg and Jan Riopelle of the Publishing Division and finally, Steven Darby who photographed the artifacts. I would also like to thank Ursula Desmarteau who edited the translated manuscript for Aubut & Associates Ltd. In addition, the exhibition project itself owes much to Senior Interpretive Planner Marie Currie who guided and supported it from the very beginning.

Finally, I wish to express my gratitude to all my colleagues in the Ethnology and Cultural Studies Division at the Canadian Museum of Civilization for their unstinting support and warm encouragement throughout the preparation of the **Beads of Life** exhibition and the writing of this book. I am particularly grateful to Carmelle Bégin who had the idea for the book, and to Andrea Laforêt and Judy Thompson who kindly read the manuscript and offered many useful suggestions.

Figure 1 Display of Ndebele dolls at the Johannesburg airport. South Africa, 2004.

Photo: Richard Labelle

INTRODUCTION

This book provides an introduction to the traditional beadwork of eastern and southern Africa based on a study of pieces from Canadian collections. It accompanies the exhibition **Beads of Life: Eastern and Southern African Adornments** which opened at the Canadian Museum of Civilization on April 14, 2005. To our knowledge, this may be the first time that an exhibition has brought together beadwork from eastern and southern Africa. It is also one of the first major exhibitions of African art to be presented by a Canadian museum in many years.

The purpose of this work is to attempt to answer general questions about eastern and southern African beadwork and to correct some of the misunderstandings that persist to this day about this little-known art form.

For several years now, beadwork from eastern and southern Africa has become more prevalent in publications dedicated to beadwork, in fashion shows or on Internet sites, and particularly in boutiques in large cities where it is sold in vast quantities both in Africa and around the world. However, until recently, beadwork was notably absent from international exhibitions of African art, relegated to the rank of a craft that was not worthy of museological attention. During the past decade, beadwork began to appear in exhibitions, as frequently in North America and Europe as in Africa.[1] This new interest is perhaps due in part to the rapidity with which the daily use of traditional dress is disappearing in Africa. It may also be attributed to the explosive renaissance of beadwork in post-apartheid South Africa, as well as to a certain attraction to lively modes of artistic expression that contrast with "classical" African art.

Nevertheless, exhibitions devoted exclusively to beadwork are rare. More often than not, beadwork serves as a complement to the sculpture of West and Central Africa, enhancing it with a touch of colour. In addition, documentation for pieces of beadwork, particularly beadwork from East Africa, is often poor. No inventory has ever been produced of holdings of eastern and southern African beadwork in the world's major museums. To further complicate matters, although the advent of markets for beadwork has helped to spread certain types of information about this art form, the information is often superficial or erroneous.

Most importantly, however, there is considerable misunderstanding about eastern and southern African beadwork, which in turn has damaged its reputation among researchers and contributed to its devaluation. The historical fact that the glass beads were introduced by European settlers, and thus not made by their African users, has not only become a major obstacle to the appreciation of objects made with beads, but has also led to confusion about the function and meaning of these works.

In her introduction to *Beads and Beadwork of East and South Africa*,[2] Margret Carey noted that although glass beads arrived in the Zulu kingdom as early as the beginning of the nineteenth century, the clothing and adornments created with these beads could not be considered "traditional" because they were made of an "introduced" material. In Carey's opinion, the expression "traditional clothing" that she uses to describe a "non-Western" outfit is thus a sort of compromise, given the recent development of this "tradition."[3] Despite the fact that the term "tradition" is, at the very least, imprecise and can refer to all kinds of historical contexts,

Carey nonetheless affirms that because of its late and "foreign" arrival, beadwork is not part of the tradition. In that case, what *is* it a part of?

In order to clear up this misunderstanding, it is necessary, first of all, to distinguish between "beadwork" as it is considered in the West, and as it is considered in eastern and southern Africa.

In the West, "beadwork" encompasses items made with glass beads of different sizes, colours and shapes. Beadwork always had an ornamental function, whether it was used on clothing or on personal objects and accessories for women, or at times for men. The tradition of beadwork stretches back several centuries in Europe where it was a pastime among girls and women in polite society. In Europe, glass beads undoubtedly replaced the natural pearls and precious and semi-precious stones that had once decorated the clothing of the elite.

African beadwork, especially the beadwork of eastern and southern Africa, is itself characterized by the use of glass beads to create ornaments and garments for daily and ceremonial use by each member of a society. This activity was formerly the responsibility of all women in a community, but in recent times, and especially with the commercial development of beadwork, it has also become a specialized activity. These items of clothing and adornment, as well as the principal beading techniques, had already existed well before the adoption of glass beads, although they were made with other materials. As a result, the beadwork produced today in eastern and southern Africa can be seen as the continuation of a tradition that has been well established since time immemorial. Although imported glass beads provoked a rush of enthusiasm upon their arrival in Africa and radically transformed the "look" of ornaments and traditional dress, they were only one of many materials used, and their adoption by African women was sometimes temporary.

The amalgamation of African beadwork with a Western craft industry having a purely ornamental purpose, and sometimes an elitist role, thus rests upon a misunderstanding that contributes to the devaluation of African beadwork by creating false ideas about what it is: that its purpose is mainly decorative, that wearing vast amounts of beadwork is a sign of wealth, and finally that this 'craft' was born when European settlers arrived in Africa, therefore suggesting that women copied it from them.

We hope to correct this misunderstanding by examining, in particular, the social and religious implications of clothing and ornaments in eastern and southern Africa. Far from being a simple recreational craft, beadwork in this area has always played an essential role in the expression of identity at both the individual and collective levels. While they remain distinct from the beadwork and clothing traditions of other major regions in Africa, the beadwork traditions of eastern and southern Africa have many points in common. One of these commonalities is that in the past, the principal function of beaded clothing and ornaments was to identify the status of individuals as well as their peer groups. This identification was linked to obligatory participation in ceremonies marking the passage from one status to another. In addition, preferences in the choice of bead colours are, or were at some time, identical in both regions, and these preferences may be based upon a desire for religious protection dating from the use of older materials of natural origin. Finally, beadwork is an exclusively feminine activity in both regions.

Chapter 1 of this book provides a short introduction to Canadian collections of African art and the cultures of eastern and southern Africa. Chapter 2 reviews the origins of beadwork through an inventory of the principal materials that were used before the arrival of glass beads, and explores their socio-religious functions. Chapter 3 examines the impact of the arrival of massive quantities of glass beads in Africa on personal ornamentation, as well as the naming and symbolic interpretations of colours. The ritual function of specific colours and its impact on the choice of certain colour combinations, as well as the organization of space in beadwork, are explained in Chapter 4, and the principal beadwork styles are enumerated. Chapter 5 contains a look at several of the more important status ornaments that mark major stages in life, including initiation, marriage, motherhood and maturity. Finally, Chapter 6 explores the reasons for the abandonment of traditional dress in eastern and southern Africa. This chapter also includes a review of contemporary forms of beadwork, especially commercial beadwork intended for the tourist market, as well as other current uses of beadwork ranging from political to commemorative.

As the creators of beaded clothing and adornments, the women of eastern and southern Africa are front and centre in this book. They are the metaphorical "weavers" of a community's social fabric. In all conditions of life, they make objects that are central to initiation rites, marriage ceremonies and all other collective activities. In this way, they affirm the status of individuals and their ties to the entire community. It is these women, who remain largely anonymous, that this work seeks to honour.

Figure 2 Maasai woman sewing beads on leather. Kenya, 1984.
Photo: Marie-Louise Labelle

Endnotes

1. Particularly in South Africa during the 1990s. See *Art and Ambiguity: Perspectives on the Brenthurst Collection of Southern African Art*; *Ezakwantu: Beadwork from the Eastern Cape*; *Zulu Treasures of Kings & Commoners: A Celebration of the Material Culture of the Zulu People*; *Convention, Context, Change*; *Ten Years of Collecting (1979–1989)*, etc.

2. Margret Carey, *Beads and Beadwork of East and South Africa*, (Shire Ethnography, U.K., 1986).

3. "While such beadwork is indeed early, it cannot be called truly traditional since it arises out of an introduced material. 'Traditional clothing' as described in the following pages is therefore a relatively recent development." Carey, 1986, p. 5.

EASTERN AND SOUTHERN AFRICAN BEADWORK FROM CANADIAN COLLECTIONS

1

The objects presented in this book have been drawn exclusively[1] from Canadian collections, including museums, universities and a few private collections. Although they are little known by the general public either in Canada or abroad, the number of objects of African origin in Canadian collections may be as high as 25,000. The Royal Ontario Museum houses the largest collection with more than 7,000 objects; the Glenbow Museum has about 6,000, followed by the Museum of Anthropology at the University of British Columbia, the Vancouver Museum, McGill University's Redpath Museum and the Canadian Museum of Civilization.

From which regions of Africa do these objects come? Central Africa, particularly the Democratic Republic of the Congo and Angola, is the area that is best represented, both in total number of pieces and in quantity of early artifacts. However, West African countries such as Nigeria, Côte d'Ivoire and Ghana are also well represented, as are East African countries such as Ethiopia, and southern African nations such as Botswana. The most under-represented African region in Canadian museological collections is North Africa.

All types of objects are included in the collections; however, their quality is uneven. Few objects were gathered by professional collectors or Africanists, and such objects are rarely part of a museum's acquisition plan. As a result, Canadian collections of African art tend to include a sizable number of objects made for commercial purposes. Others are damaged, and many are severely lacking in documentation. Nonetheless, several of the collections that were acquired about a century ago include numerous pieces of great ethnographic and aesthetic value.

Since the 1970's UNESCO Convention on the Means of Prohibiting and Preventing the Illicit Export, Import and Transfer of Ownership of Cultural Property, as well as restrictions imposed on the exportation of materials from protected animal species such as ivory, many Canadian museums have refused to acquire objects without proof that they were imported into Canada prior to these regulations. In addition, because Canadian museums generally do not have acquisition budgets for objects of African origin, the expansion of these collections relies almost entirely on donations. Furthermore, since most museums do not currently have curators of African Arts and Cultures, few museum staff are in a position to judge the authenticity and quality of pieces in their collections. Finally, since the majority of ethnology departments at Canada's major museological institutions are dedicated to the study of Canada's First Peoples, the development of African collections has not been a priority. African collections in Canadian museums are therefore in a precarious position, lacking specialists to study, document or display them, or make new acquisitions.

Many African objects in Canadian collections have not benefited from the advances in research on the anthropology of art that occurred throughout the twentieth century. As a result, the interest of museum professionals and the general public has not evolved significantly since the objects were originally acquired. This in turn means that many of these objects continue to evoke a mysterious primitiveness from which a large number of people prefer to distance themselves.

On the other hand, because of increased immigration to Canada from Africa and the Caribbean, these artifacts have acquired new political significance. Among certain community spokespersons, they have become the focus of symbolic claims that have led to attempts to re-appropriate the discussion from non-African curators. Until the late 1990s, this situation tended to render both sides — the Black community and museum staff — respectively suspicious and nervous, to say the least, of any exhibition idea involving African collections. That situation, however, is now beginning to change. In 2004, the National Gallery of Canada presented an exhibition of African art.[2] In 2005, it is believed for the first time in the history of Canadian museums, the Royal Ontario Museum advertised for the position of Cultural Anthropologist specializing in Africa. Finally, in 2006, some months after the opening of **Beads of Life** at the Canadian Museum of Civilization, the Royal Ontario Museum will open a permanent gallery devoted to African art. These new exhibitions should help reveal Africa's cultural riches to the Canadian public and trigger new projects for the future.

Objects in Canadian collections from eastern and southern Africa number about 7,000, or slightly less than one-third of all African objects in these collections. Once again, the Royal Ontario Museum leads the way, housing more than 2,000 artifacts with this provenance.[3] The countries of eastern and southern Africa represented in these collections are Sudan, Ethiopia, Somalia, Kenya, Uganda, Rwanda, Tanzania, Malawi, Zambia, Zimbabwe, Mozambique, Namibia, Botswana, South Africa, Swaziland and Lesotho.

The organizations or individuals who brought these collections to Canadian museums and universities are from all walks of life and rarely represent a stereotypical "Canadian collector." These collections, however, certainly have much to say about a century of relations between Canada and Africa. Several trends emerge: collections resulting from military interventions (for instance the South African War of 1899 to 1902); from interactions between local populations and missionaries and colonials; from interactions of an economic, diplomatic, humanitarian, or scientific nature; or from tourism and international development. Several collectors stand out due to their roles in Canadian history or in scientific research, but taken together, the sources comprise a cross-section of Canadian society.

Often, particularly in the case of older collections from the late nineteenth and early twentieth centuries, the circumstances of their acquisition in Africa are unknown. This has occurred for a number of reasons. Sometimes a distant or long-deceased member of the donor family collected the objects. In other cases, the donor's identity is not known, or the location and exact circumstances of collection were ignored or not recorded. Sometimes the object was purchased in a shop in Africa or elsewhere. And in some cases, the object was acquired directly by the museum from an art dealer, or perhaps transferred from another museum.

Only through assiduous detective work can we retrace the history of these objects and their collection. This issue is not limited to Canada and concerns a large number of African works in museums around the world. It is, however, by no means certain that retracing the circumstances of collection will enable us to learn more about the object, since information related to the date and place of collection is precisely what is most often lacking. Similarly, research into the biographies of the collectors, with the exception of a few anthropologists or notable collectors with a documented history, may contribute little to our knowledge of the objects.

What are these objects? Among early collections, the number of weapons is impressive: spears, shields, bows, arrows and quivers, swords, knives of all shapes and sizes, axes, clubs and staffs, all of which no doubt fascinated European and Canadian collectors of the late nineteenth and early twentieth centuries who brought them back as "trophies." The Royal Ontario Museum, in particular, has a large number of spears and shields from East Africa (Ethiopia and Kenya), many of which are of remarkable quality. The collections also abound in the tools of daily life including agricultural implements, baskets, matting, pots, wooden spoons and bowls, calabashes and several musical instruments. Canadians also brought back a wide range of souvenir objects: animals made of ivory, miniature baskets, wooden sculptures of animals and human figures, beadwork and replicas of Western objects. The age of some of these pieces suggests that production of such objects for tourists is as old as European colonization in Africa, and perhaps even older. Many of these objects were made at missions and were intended to demonstrate the skills of African artisans and workers. These souvenirs often display a caricatured representation of Africa: the "chief," the "wise elder," the "warrior," or the nearly nude young woman, meant to reflect "typical" members of African societies, stereotypes that were interchangeable from one society to another.

Finally, the collections also include personal objects. These range from tobacco accessories (pipes, snuffboxes, spoons, etc.) to clothing and adornments to "fertility" dolls, headrests and carved wooden staffs. This last grouping reveals a particular characteristic. Many of the personal objects in Canadian collections were once used by the societies that produced them. This can be seen from their obvious signs of wear, as well as the traces of red ochre and fat that remain on them. By and large, these items are not only remarkable in quality, but are frequently quite old as well. They convey valuable information about the people living in eastern and southern Africa from the late nineteenth to the late twentieth centuries. From north to south, the principal countries from which these personal objects come are Sudan, Ethiopia, Kenya, Tanzania, Zimbabwe, Botswana and South Africa. Objects from other countries such as Uganda, Rwanda and Burundi are not present in sufficient numbers in Canadian collections to be part of our selection, although these countries have certainly produced extensive amounts of beadwork at various times in their history.

In view of the significant role that chance has played in the way these objects were collected, and the fact that certain historical and economic circumstances contributed to the arrival of large quantities of objects of a certain provenance to the detriment of others, it is inevitable that gaps will be present within the collections. Certain cultures and periods are relatively well represented; others are nearly or completely absent from the collections. In addition, many objects bear witness to particular choices by those who acquired them, for whom one of the first concerns, if we exclude objects gathered by anthropologists and a few experienced collectors, was to bring back an "exotic" souvenir of the Africa in which they had briefly lived, or through which they had passed. Few among them would have been able to detect the particular ethnographic or aesthetic value of the objects they acquired. Moreover, many of their "collections" were dependent on well-established markets at which only certain types of objects were available for sale to foreigners living in an urban milieu.

Beadwork tends to be found on the bottom rung in the collection of African objects. It seems of lesser interest to collectors than sculpture or weapons (spears, shields, clubs, swords, bows and arrows), which appear to have taken centre stage. Because the beads were imported from Europe, beadwork is considered a Western type of craft without great "authenticity," that is to say, without the "exotic" touch expected from Africa. In addition, since most collectors are unable to detect the line between beadwork made to be worn and beadwork made for sale, the temptation is great to deny value to all works of beading. Furthermore, beadwork is considered a feminine activity and therefore lacks, among male collectors in particular, the prestige of African sculpture that was created by men for sacred purposes. Finally, the collection of these objects is of no practical use since most of the clothing and adornments made with traditional beads can neither be displayed on the walls of the home, nor worn by their purchasers because of the difficulty of combining them with Western-style clothes. Thus, once the collected objects are removed from their context, they have no real purpose and are frequently abandoned to their fate in a trunk at the back of an attic, or donated to a museum.

Taken out of context, these disparate objects become opaque fragments of information, to which an inventory produced for the **Beads of Life** exhibition project has succeeded in giving a semblance of logic, in terms of their provenances, functions and styles. Consultations with Canadians from eastern and southern Africa have further helped to place certain objects in time and space. The various reactions we received from community members demonstrate the sometimes insurmountable distance that exists between these collections and the reality of contemporary Africa. Witnesses of another time, and at times violent relations between the West and Africa, they sometimes elicited reserved reactions on the part of this community. The "mixed feelings" expressed by Kuwee Kumsa of Oromo origin are a good example. She was overjoyed to discover authentic objects bearing witness to the history of her people, but at the same time, she was saddened because she could not have access to them and had to be content with copies when she organized some traditional ceremonies within her Toronto community. Her problem arose from the fact that she did not know how to identify with these objects, or how to link them to her own past or to that of her ancestors: "How do I relate to this now? Is it me, is it not me?"[4] The part that chance played in their collection, prompted by motives unrelated to them, or that reflected past or recent African history, was suddenly thrown into stark relief during visits by members of this community to the CMC storerooms. For some individuals, however, the objects brought back much more vivid memories of traditions they had either witnessed or in which they had taken part. Many people also brought along personal objects that still played an active role or evoked a memory in their daily lives. These particular participants helped to provide a measure of precise information on many of the objects.

Available documentation on beadwork from eastern and southern Africa is limited. Interest in this art form is fairly recent and few studies have been exclusively devoted to it. Sources of information on ornaments a century old, or older, are rarer still. It thus becomes necessary to rely upon descriptions provided by the first explorers in Africa, or on anthropological mono-graphs detailing the political, religious and economic spheres of the cultures in question. Neither type of work contains much information on the ways in which people reshaped and adorned their bodies, nor on the way this marked tendency in eastern and southern Africa could be closely related to their particular areas of research interest.

The making of beaded adornments is not limited to eastern and southern Africa. Other cultures in Nigeria, Cameroon, the Democratic Republic of the Congo and Mali used glass beads for their adornments, or continue to use them today. However, it is a particular practice in many societies of eastern and southern Africa to make adornments with glass beads, just as the carving of masks and figures is similarly rare. The tradition of mask making, in particular, is virtually absent in eastern and southern Africa, except in certain societies such as in Malawi and Tanzania.

A certain degree of homogeneity in the function and style of objects from eastern and southern Africa indicates cultural constants along an imaginary line from north to south. From the Dinka of the southern Sudan, to the Xhosa of the Eastern Cape, through the Oromo, Maasai, and Zulu, there exists the same families of personal objects that take the form of beaded jewellery, leather skirts embroidered with beads, wooden headrests or delicately ornamented snuffboxes.

These cultures, however, are all quite distinct. From north to south, they include societies of the following language groups: Nilotic (the Dinka, Turkana, Samburu and Maasai), Cushitic (the Oromo, Afar, Somali and Iraqw), Bantu (the Kikuyu, Kamba, Tonga, Tsonga, Shona, Zulu, Ndebele and Xhosa), and finally Khoisan (the San).[5] These societies constitute a fraction of the hundreds of cultures in eastern and southern Africa, but it is primarily among these societies that beadwork is practised extensively. This practice arose as a result of the particular structure of clothing and jewellery produced before the arrival of beads, adornments that are themselves evidence of common cultural traits throughout eastern and southern Africa, and that override differences of language, economic activity and historical circumstance.

These cultural traits include pastoralism, the male system of age classification with its initiation ceremonies and rites of passage, the absence of a centralized power in favour of the guidance of elders, and finally, among confirmed pastoralists, nomadism or semi-nomadism. Livestock plays a central role in pastoral societies, not only because it provides essential food and forms the basis for a system of exchanges and gifts, but also because animals play an important part in ceremonies and rituals. Even among sedentary agricultural societies, particularly in South Africa (Zulu, Xhosa), livestock assumes a strong symbolic importance. This common attachment to livestock gives rise to certain communal economic trends that in turn determine the particular use of certain materials, and by extension, the creation of similar styles of adornment. Ultimately, certain specific social systems pave the way for particular aesthetic choices, while certain ways of life lead to the production of specific types of functional objects. Pastoralism, for example, whether or not it is combined with a nomadic way of life, demands that personal and utilitarian objects be designed for easy transport. Thus, pastoral peoples do not produce sculptures or large items of furniture, but rather objects that can be easily loaded onto the back of a donkey or camel, including sometimes the entire framing structures of their homes (Somali, Oromo). By the same token, objects are rarely kept when unused. For practical reasons, many of these societies cannot afford to accumulate material objects. Objects that have sustained too much damage are sold or destroyed, and materials such as glass beads carefully salvaged to make something new.

Figure 3 Livestock is at the centre of economic, social and religious activities among pastoral peoples. Northern Kenya, 1990.

Photo: Marie-Louise Labelle

Another characteristic of many of these societies is the tendency to pass objects from person to person. They are the subject of constant transactions, as donations or friendly loans, and as gifts between family members or lovers. The object itself is not valued in the same way as in Western societies. Its sole value lies in what it represents, that is, a bond between different people maintaining a specific relationship. This has given rise to the misunderstanding that often exists between the way in which we, as Westerners, consider these objects, and what they represented in the lives of their creators and users.

One of the notable misconceptions related to these objects is their character as "unique pieces." In eastern and southern Africa, all members of the community participated in the creation of ornaments and personal objects; the range of skill thus varied from one individual to another. Under such conditions, no object is truly "characteristic" of a particular style, and must be studied within the context of a series of similar objects. This makes it possible for us to identify aesthetic rules while still noting the particular nuances resulting from the maker's individual preferences.

Several historical, economic and social factors have contributed to the fact that a large number of societies, particularly those of East Africa, have long preserved their traditional dress and, in many cases, continue to do so today. Traditional dress played a critical role in these societies. In West Africa, for example, it was often a sign of prestige and seen as a royal insignia, whereas in eastern and southern Africa it was a form of "identity card" for each individual, and fulfilled very precise roles at the personal and social levels. The wearing of certain traditional

Figure 4 Ndebele painted house. South Africa, 1990s.
Photo: Mark Lewis

clothing was strongly linked to social behaviours within which fundamental religious principles came into play. Thus, its abandonment does not represent an act as innocent as removing a necklace of beads from one's neck: it is an obvious sign of the individual's renunciation, whether final or temporary, of traditional social values. It is a process within which a great many social and historical changes must be taken into account, and upon which movements involving the wearing of traditional costume for economic and/or political ends have been grafted, causing, at least outwardly,[6] a reversal in direction.

The conditions under which adornments are created differ somewhat from north to south. Notwithstanding the fact that the cultures of southern Africa had much earlier access to glass beads due to their historical circumstances, the use of beads in the southern Sudan or Ethiopia, for example, is quite distinct from that of South Africa. Access to glass beads was more limited for some peoples of East Africa, in particular those of the Horn of Africa, both because of their late entry into a market economy, and above all, because of their geographic distance from major urban centres due to their pastoral and nomadic ways of life.

For these reasons, beads made of glass appear in more limited numbers in the North, and beading techniques are, in certain cases, more rudimentary. On the other hand, more of the peoples in East Africa have maintained their use of the traditional costume for the same reasons as those noted above: their remoteness from urban centres and their nomadism. A number of traditional adornments made with original materials are still produced today in East Africa, although they have disappeared in the southern region. Still other groups have reinforced their use of the traditional costume in reaction to an external threat; others have maintained it for commercial reasons (tourism), although in this case, the function and appearance of the costume have been completely modified. These historical differences have helped to produce the stylistic variations that can be found from north to south.

Today's beadwork adornments are a direct continuation of items that existed prior to the arrival of massive quantities of glass beads. These adornments were made with materials available in the environment, which were in turn the products of the central economic activities of these societies. The choice of materials was based upon the effectiveness of their properties, whether of a protective nature, or indicative of social status. In order to learn how to "read" the beadwork adornments of today, we must become familiar with the materials and adornments that preceded them.

Endnotes

1. With the exception of the Iraqw shirt from the Indianapolis Museum of Art, borrowed to replace the shirt from the Royal Ontario Museum that was unavailable for the **Beads of Life** exhibition.

2. **Material Differences: Art and Identity in Africa**. September 17, 2004 to January 2, 2005.

3. It is closely followed by the Museum of Anthropology at the University of British Columbia, the Vancouver Museum, the Glenbow Museum, the Redpath Museum, the Anthropology Department of the Université de Montréal, etc.

4. "I wanted these objects and I could never find them. Even back home they are not there. So I said, 'Oh, this is wonderful: somebody has recovered them.' Somewhere there I can relate to that, that's me, I discovered an aspect of me. But then I said, 'Oh my God! How could I not have it and these people could have it you know?' It is a mixed feeling. I was very happy and I was also sad because I don't have it but somebody else has it. How did they get here? How is it that I couldn't find it, but it's me?" Kuwee Kumsa, Research Assistant/Consultant for **Beads of Life**, Oromo culture, interviewed on April 25, 2003 at the Canadian Museum of Civilization.

5. For the sake of simplicity, the word "San" is used in a generic fashion throughout this book.

6. See Chapter 6.

MATERIALS OF EARLY ORNAMENT AND CLOTHING

2

What remains today of traditional dress in eastern and southern Africa appears to have little in common with the dress described by early explorers of the eighteenth and nineteenth centuries. In reality, the structure of traditional clothing and the way in which it reshapes the body have remained fairly similar, but most of the materials used to make traditional garments have changed, definitively altering their appearance. A voyage back in time is necessary to better understand the traditional dress still worn today in eastern and southern Africa and to determine which forms and essential elements have survived the overwhelming influx of western materials such as glass beads. Some of the adornments and clothing made of older materials and featured in the **Beads of Life** exhibition are still in use today, particularly in East Africa. Others have disappeared and examples of these objects only remain in a few museums. Certain materials did not disappear entirely with the arrival of glass beads, but continued to be used, together with newer materials, to make clothing and items of adornment carrying messages essential to the proper functioning of society.

The exploration and subsequent colonization of eastern and southern Africa brought drastic economic and historical upheavals that had a lasting impact on the way people clothed and adorned themselves. The major difference between the traditional-style clothing and ornaments worn today, and those of the pre-colonial period, is that the latter were created mostly from locally available materials.

These materials included wood, grasses, seeds, shells, materials from wild and domesticated animals such as skins, hooves, bone, ivory, horn and feathers, and above all, metals such as iron. Materials not available in the immediate environment were obtained through trade with neighbouring peoples. Some peoples specialized in the production of finished materials such as metal chains or thick metal wire, or in the provision of unfinished materials such as ivory, and were paid in livestock or other products. From time immemorial, beads made of glass, brought by caravans of Arab merchants from the shores of the Indian Ocean, reached even the remotest regions of eastern and southern Africa. These beads remained rare however, and thus were used sparingly. Prior to the widespread adoption of glass beads, people made beads from seeds, wood, teeth, bone, cowries, ostrich eggs, clay and metal. The time and care spent in their creation made these beads objects of considerable value.

What is striking in nineteenth and early twentieth century photographs depicting people dressed in traditional dress in East Africa is the apparent uniformity of costume between cultures as different as the Kamba, the Kikuyu and the Maasai. The materials used to make garments were, in fact, common to all, and different groups frequently wore identical items of adornment. Sometimes, these items even served the same function. This often makes it difficult to differentiate between the various groups, since the majority wore metal ornaments including thick brass and iron wire encircling the limbs and neck, earrings and necklaces made of chains, and skin clothing decorated with metal, cowries or ostrich egg shell beads. Only a good knowledge of the principal characteristics of their ornamentation enables us to distinguish between these groups. This apparent uniformity was broken ultimately by the adoption of glass beads and cotton fabrics. From that moment on, cultural and regional differences became visible through newly distinct choices of colour combinations and patterns.[1]

In South Africa, the use of local materials is poorly documented in photographs because the widespread adoption of glass beads occurred earlier in this region than in eastern Africa. Consequently, even sketches by the region's earliest explorers are of little help in this regard. Although often depicting people's attire, they do not show the appearance of traditional dress prior to the adoption of beads. Instead, the sketches show women and men wearing ornaments that are already highly coloured and composed primarily of red, blue and white beads. Photographs dating from the end of the nineteenth century depict young Zulus decked out in apparently excessive amounts of beadwork. Most of these photographs were taken in studios and the models were "costumed" for the occasion.[2] We therefore have a very limited idea of the garments and ornaments that were worn in daily life. In addition, these photographs correspond to a key historical period in which beads were no longer exclusively for royal use and had spread into the general population. Thus, only the written accounts of the first explorers in South Africa can give us an idea of the nature of the materials used for adornments and clothing before the adoption of glass beads. These were probably made from the skins of wild and domestic animals, plant fibres, wood, shells and animal materials of all sorts, as well as metal.

Clothing and adornments made with earlier materials were "alive." They were scented (aromatic grasses, sheep fat, etc.), often noisy (the jingle of bracelets, anklets and chains, and the rustle of skirts along the ground, etc.), and, showing signs of wear and age, they matured at the same time as their users. Above all, they were "talkative": they provided an immediate visual indication of family, social, political and ritual status, and even the wearer's personal history. Marked with a certain severity compared with their lighter and more highly-coloured successors, the adornments and clothing of earlier days, as well as the materials from which they were made, assumed a quasi-religious importance. Their beauty went hand in hand with conformity to sometimes rigid codes of life, the origins of which are lost in the myths of creation. These fundamental principles also dictated the rules of behaviour between the different genders and age sets. Clothing and items of adornment, as well as the materials from which they were made, were also dependent upon this hierarchical structure. They obliged all members of a society to reflect acceptance of the social order and the assorted rights and privileges of their rank and status, and also to confirm this acceptance in their physical appearance. In some societies, prophets or diviners could even demand that the entire community wear particular clothing and ornaments in response to prescriptions received from God.[3] Certain ornaments revealed the humble position of a married woman within her husband's family, the differentiation between young people and elders, the role of spokespersons and diviners, and the importance of social divisions in general. Above all, these items and the materials from which they were made were only a part of the ensemble of elements that played a protective role in the ritual cycle throughout the difficult passages of life, of which initiation was the most important. These elements were of animal, plant and mineral origin, and were either prominently displayed or carefully concealed. They bore witness to the individual's successful participation in different rites of passage. In fact, almost every item of clothing and adornment was worn only after the individual had undergone a ceremonial proceeding or taken an active part in private or public events that included ritual activities.

The issues involving adornment in southern and eastern Africa are altogether different from the notion of adornment as "finery," i.e. something having a purely aesthetic role, as in the West, or, as is often written about African beadwork, reflecting the wealth of its owner.

To properly understand how the idea of "beauty" is expressed and interpreted from the southern Sudan to the tip of the Cape in the cultures represented here, it is necessary to explore certain philosophical concepts specific to these cultures. For many of them, the notion of "beauty" is interchangeable with that of "good." "Good" is understood in the sense of what is "socially acceptable." The main function of ornaments and clothing was thus to make the wearer appear socially acceptable, not to display individual preferences of a purely decorative nature. This of course does not exclude personal creativity, in all its variety.

Each culture had very precise notions about what is socially acceptable or unacceptable, and quite often the words that defined the criteria of physical appearance were the same as those used to define moral qualities. For example, to qualify colours or clothing combinations, the Maasai use the terms *kenare* and *kemakua*, which are also words commonly used to judge acts that do or do not conform to codes of conduct and interpersonal relations, based on the notion of *enkanyit* (respect). Thus, placing an orange bead next to a red bead, for example, is *kemakua*, "unacceptable," but placing a red bead near a green one is *kenare*, "acceptable." Mixing modern clothing with traditional, or wearing clothing that does not correspond to one's status or gender is also *kemakua*, "unacceptable." In the same way, the terms *sidai* and *torrono*, when applied to personal appearance, are better translated as "good" and "bad" respectively, rather than as "beautiful" or "ugly."[4]

Among many peoples of the Nilotic or Cushitic language groups, the aesthetic assumed a religious dimension, applying not only to the body and its finery, but to all of the environment, physical (nature, livestock appearance, etc.) and social (codes of conduct in daily life and ceremonies, oratory arts, song, dance, etc.).

According to Aneesa Kassam, who has done extensive fieldwork among the Oromo, the adornments of the Oromo of Kenya and Ethiopia "belong to the category of *waan aadaa* or 'things of tradition,' and thus have a deep religious significance for the Oromo. For both men and women, they crown personal and social achievement, manhood and motherhood, which are seen ultimately as a form of praise in honour of *Waaqa*, the Oromo Supreme Deity."[5]

This was true, for example, of the Dinka of the southern Sudan. Francis Deng identifies a crucial Dinka principle called *cieng*. The *cieng* defined behaviour, morals, traditions and human relations. But the verb *cieng* also implied the wearing of clothing and ornaments, which clearly places physical appearance in a purely moral category.[6]

In addition, again according to Francis Deng, "honour, dignity, and inner pride as well as their outward appearance and bearing are part of what the Dinka call *dheeng* … Initiation ceremonies, celebrations of marriage, the decoration of 'personality oxen', dancing, indeed any personal demonstration of an aesthetic or sensuous quality is considered *dheeng*. The way a man walks, runs, talks, eats, or dresses expresses his *dheeng*. As a noun, *dheeng* means such things as dignity, beauty, nobility, handsomeness, elegance, charm, grace, gentleness, richness, hospitality, generosity, and kindness … *adheng* … is often used to mean 'a gentleman.'"[7] Consequently,

Figure 5 Among the Dinka, the principle of *dheeng* defined moral character as well as physical appearance, including personal decoration and clothing. Young Dinka woman, Sudan, early 1950s.

Photo: Hulton Archive, Getty Images

the idea that wearing a great quantity of ornaments is intended to flaunt material riches makes no sense in a social context in which the qualities of an individual were measured, first and foremost, against moral criteria. Within such a context, displaying personal wealth would have been a matter of pure provocation. This is true as well for many other societies in eastern and southern Africa.

Among the Zulu and the Xhosa, the wearing of traditional dress was also associated with moral principles. Erich Bigalke notes that during Xhosa ceremonies, many young people took particular satisfaction in knowing they were more nicely dressed than others: "A well-dressed person has dignity, is respected, loveable and an object of attention. One girl believed that a well-turned-out person could compensate for unfortunate physical attributes: 'Many ugly *abafana* (young initiated men) and boys have a lot of girl friends because they dress nicely.'"[8]

Among the Zulu, a young bride was required to wear certain clothing and adornments as a sign of respect for her in-laws. This attitude of respect is defined by the term *hlonipha*. Xhosa women also observed these obligations. *Hlonipha* describes wide-ranging aspects of the

Figure 6 The hairstyle and head ornaments of this married Zulu woman express respect for her in-laws. South Africa, late 19th century.

Photo: H. N. Hutchinson. *The Living Races of Mankind,* 1901 communication and behaviour of a young wife towards her in-laws, including the correct language to be used in their presence.[9] Specific ornaments helped the wife to fulfill her *hlonipha* obligations and maintain a good relationship with her husband's ancestors.[10] A woman had to conceal her body, shoulders and head, and she wore a headband made of fibres (*umnqwazi*) around her hair, or a hat to shield her eyes. She was also required to keep her eyes lowered in the presence of her in-laws. As she aged, she was released from these obligations, save those related to language.[11]

Ornaments, clothing and personal objects were so important in an individual's existence that many were either destroyed at death, buried with the deceased, or passed on to the closest relative (son, daughter, husband, wife, etc.), who wore them temporarily or permanently.[12] During mourning, the relatives of the deceased were obliged to undergo physical transformations including shaving, smearing the body and face with a mixture of white chalk and water or refraining from wearing their habitual red ochre body paint. They also ceased wearing their ornaments, thus temporarily erasing their social status.[13] It was only following several purification rituals that their usual finery could be adopted again.

In addition, diviners and healers of eastern and southern Africa used their costume to communicate directly with God or the ancestors' spirits, either through particular colours in their clothing or ornaments,[14] or through elements linking them to the world of their ancestors and to the rites they had to perform to enable them to assume their supernatural duties.[15] Numerous elements came into play: bones, the gallbladders of animals sacrificed during initiation as a diviner, the skins or vertebrae of snakes, cowries, stones, leather sandals, plant powders, tobacco, glass beads, etc. (Figure 7).

The body itself, which was both a canvas for the application of body paint, scarring, decorative burns, etc. and a support for ornaments and clothing, was charged with messages. In fact, the name given to particular items of adornment provided information on the importance accorded to the part of the body on which they were worn, sites specifically chosen for the delivery of certain messages linked to status and age. Two essential parts of the body, the head and waist, were involved in the communication of messages. The hair, ears and neck were reserved for the application of specific ornaments and makeup. The hair was a privileged medium in eastern and southern Africa. Each modification in appearance that it underwent showed the person's acquisition of status or a particular state of being, knowledge of which had to be conveyed to the community since changes to an individual's status required

Figure 7 It is likely that a diviner wore this necklace featuring charms of animal origin.

Necklace
South Africa
Late 19th or early 20th century
Glass beads, horn, claws, reptile skin, bone, wood, brass button, animal hide and plant fibre
23 cm (l) x 14 cm (w)
Provincial Museum of Alberta, Edmonton H62.12.926
Photo: © Canadian Museum of Civilization, Steven Darby

that specific behaviour be adopted by others when in that person's presence. Changes in status might include initiation that was underway or already completed, illness, marriage, motherhood, mourning, the capacity for divination, and the status of leader. Hair was either shaved or left long, shaped into a cone, braided, smeared with red ochre or ashes, and dressed with various ornaments. Hair was also the subject of various taboos. Among the Samburu and the Maasai, for example, only uninitiated young girls could touch the long, braided hair of the *morans*, or young initiated men (Figure 8).

The earlobes were also a preferred location for the communication of important messages related to status. From infancy to death, successive ornaments were inserted into the pierced lobe, which thus became stretched and enlarged in order to relate a person's life story, including

Figure 8 Long hair is often a sign of a particular status. Samburu *moran* (initiated young man). Kenya, 1985.
Photo: Marie-Louise Labelle

initiation, marriage, motherhood/fatherhood and the wisdom of old age. Finally, the neck was adorned with quantities of necklaces that not only indicated status, but also provided information on a person's relationships with relatives. Occasionally, such necklaces also contained protective charms. In this latter case, the elements revealing more intimate information could be discreetly concealed beneath other ornaments.

The waist took on a slightly different although similar significance since adornments worn here were sometimes concealed, and concerned what was happening, literally, in the depths of a person's being. This was particularly true for young girls who wore belts and aprons that enhanced their seductiveness by revealing as well as concealing their charms. It was also true of mothers who wore belts displaying their maternity both during pregnancy and after giving birth.

The limbs were not forgotten in the delivery of messages, with an entire series of bracelets that were made of metal, horn or ivory and wood, and worn by men and women alike to show their status as spouses, mothers, respected elders and leaders.

Each of these adornments and items of clothing existed only in the context of the relationship in form and meaning that they maintained with one another. The forms created by clothing and ornaments complemented each other harmoniously, redefining the lines of the body by accentuating or concealing them. The materials also complemented one another, forming thoughtfully considered contrasts. This costume was a veritable communication system in which each element combined with others to create a "book" containing the individual's history. At each stage of maturity and acquisition of status, the book was updated. The elements of costume were in perpetual motion. Some disappeared or were transformed, and new elements appeared, sometimes for a few days only (indicators of participation in ceremonies, elements of protection against illness or temporary states, loans or gifts from a loved one, etc.).

Items of adornment were thus "heavy," both literally and figuratively: the materials from which they were made were sometimes uncomfortable, even painful to wear, and they were also indiscreet, as they revealed the personal and intimate life of the individual to the entire group.

The way in which ornaments were named sometimes indicated what was most important to members of a community. They were named by their materials, by the part of the body on which they were placed (often the two indicators were combined), and occasionally by the technique used to create them, their forms, or even the movements or sounds they produced. For example, "iron" (*esekenkei*) was the name given to an ornament made of thick iron wire worn around the neck by a married Maasai woman. Similarly, "brass" (*esurutiai*) was the name of an ornament made of two brass spirals, which was the prerogative in Kenya, not only of married women, but also of men of status.[16] The name of the part of the body on which the object was placed was simply added to make a distinction between different ornaments: *esekenkei lemurt* ("the iron wire of the neck") or *esurutiai lenkaina* ("the brass wire of the arm"). The "necklace of thombothi wood" (*umgexo wonthombothi*) was a Zulu necklace made of this material, just as certain ivory earrings worn by the Samburu were called "ivory of the ears" (*lala loonkiyia*, or literally, "elephant teeth of the ear"). The "strips of skin of the legs" (*inkeenda loolkejek*) designated anklets on a leather base worn by Maasai young people. Similarly, the traditional headdress of Maasai *morans* decorated with ostrich feathers was simply called *esidai* or "ostrich," and Turkana necklaces featuring beads made of ostrich egg were called *ngakirim* or "ostrich egg." Occasionally, it was the movement of the ornament that was indicated in its name, such as the *isiheshe* of young Zulu girls that undulated during dances and produced a rattling sound. The particular form of an ornament could also come into play, as in the *inkalulungani* of the Maasai, which were anklets made of iron, the name of which was derived from a verb meaning "that which is round." Colour did not appear to play a significant role in the names of traditional adornments.

As a general rule, however, the name of an ornament most often reflected the material from which it was made. It was the material that delivered information about the wearer, and above all provided protection during difficult passages in life, whether against the "evil eye" or any other external threat that might disturb physical and mental equilibrium. Among these materials, there were some that were particularly important.

Metal is in all likelihood the material that was once most widely used for ornaments. Iron, copper, brass and, more recently, aluminum were worked by blacksmiths for items of adornment, although they were used primarily in the making of utensils, tools and weapons (spears, knives, axes, etc.). Each society of eastern and southern Africa had its "caste" of blacksmiths who shared common characteristics. Their trade was handed down from father to son and they were generally segregated from the rest of society. In East Africa, a blacksmith's activities were traditionally viewed with suspicion, since for pastoral societies, all work involving digging the ground was considered impure. The fact that blacksmiths made weapons designed to kill no doubt contributed to this isolation. When the Maasai obtained weapons from a blacksmith, they greased their hands to protect themselves against iron's impurity. Marriages with blacksmiths' families were avoided, the number of livestock they were allowed to own was limited, and their participation in ceremonial cycles was restricted. Their work was considered "unclean" as were the places in which they operated. In Ethiopia, ironworkers were feared because of their magical powers and blacksmiths and metalworkers lived apart from the village. People were afraid of them, believing that they could cast the evil eye.[17] In the Oromo culture of Ethiopia, iron was considered a dangerous material, linked to thunder and death. Their blacksmiths were therefore of Konso origin, a neighbouring ethnic group. Iron could protect against evil forces, and could also represent "strength, divine power and resistance."[18] Among the Dinka of the southern Sudan as well, blacksmiths did not own livestock and were regarded with contempt.[19]

As was seen with the Zulu, blacksmiths were also segregated in South Africa, and their hereditary profession was limited to particular clans. The blacksmith's status was ambiguous, however, because he was both elevated and set apart from society. Communication with the ancestors contributed to the success of the production of iron, and rites were observed before and after work by the blacksmiths. "Smiths' work was associated with *umnyama*, a dark, mystical force, both powerful and dangerous, which is also associated with death, witchcraft and mystical pollution arising from various life crises … Smiths, even those involved in forging only and not smelting, were thus a potential danger to other people, who tended to avoid them and their working areas. They needed to undergo cleansing rites to release them back into their normal lives after a working session."[20]

The role of blacksmiths, first in southern and later in eastern Africa, diminished with the arrival of the Europeans who brought metals that had already been worked, thus competing with the blacksmiths' livelihood. Iron, brass and copper arrived in the form of wires of varying thicknesses that were ready for immediate use. In the making of ornaments, thick wire of iron

Figure 9

Photo: © Canadian Museum of Civilization, Steven Darby

Left:

Ishungu

Snuff Container

Zulu?, South Africa

Late 19th or early 20th century

Gourd, brass and wood

6.19 cm (h), 9.85 cm (d)

Vancouver Museum FE43 (F98)

Right:

Ishungu

Snuff Container

Zulu?, South Africa

Late 19th or early 20th century

Gourd, copper, brass and wood

6 cm (h), 6.5 cm (d)

Redpath Museum, Montreal 04973ab

Figure 10

Ixhama

Belt

Zulu, South Africa

Late 19th or early 20th century

Brass buttons, glass beads and plant fibre

79.7 cm (l) x 7.4 cm (w)

Museum of Anthropology, University of British Columbia, Vancouver 1251/2

Photo: © Canadian Museum of Civilization, Steven Darby

or brass was undoubtedly one of the most commonly used elements in eastern and southern Africa prior to the arrival of beads. The blacksmith coiled this thick wire several times around legs and arms, especially those of girls and women. It was not removed, and created lasting skin lesions.[21] Ndebele and Maasai women, in particular, wore them daily. Iron chains, widely used in a large number of East African cultures, were made by specialized artisans such as the Kamba blacksmiths in Kenya, and could be found in earrings, necklaces, bracelets and belts.

In "Prestige Ornaments: The Use of Brass in the Zulu Kingdom," C. G. Kennedy points out the extensive use that the Zulu seemed to have made of brass. Most of their personal objects were decorated with very fine copper and brass wire (Figure 9). As some of these items were elitist in nature, only the king, his wives, close advisors, and a few notable warriors were allowed to use or wear them. Body ornaments included brass rings worn on the head and around the neck and limbs. These rings were at times impossible to wear, primarily because the metal became scorching hot in hot weather. The *ubedu* was a flat, brass ring worn by the chiefs; the *umnaka* was worn by men and women of high rank, and was made of one or several round rings. The brass rings known as *amasongo*, which encircled the arms, were also reserved for the elite, as was the *ingxotha*, a wide band for the forearm. Married women attached to the royal court wore a decorative brass element in the form of a pierced ball threaded around the neck (*indondo*).[22]

All of these status-indicating ornaments disappeared with the collapse of royalty. Certain brass ornaments, however, survived into the twentieth century, including the flexible *ubusenga* rings that adorned people's limbs from the late nineteenth century on, and the *iqhosha* brass studs, first made locally and later replaced by brass buttons of European origin. These studs or buttons were used primarily to decorate the *isigcayi* "maternity

Figure 11 Several East African peoples once used iron necklaces such as this one.

Necklace
Maasai or Kikuyu, Kenya
End of the 19th century
Iron
10.16 cm (l), 12.7 cm (external diameter)
Royal Ontario Museum, Toronto 960.69.268
With the permission of the Royal Ontario Museum © ROM

Figure 12 Maasai women made their presence known through the jingling of the *inkalulungani*, which were required ornaments for married women.

Inkalulungani
Anklets
Maasai, Kenya
Second half of the 20th century
Iron, copper and aluminum
Each: 10.5 cm (diameter) x 2.1 cm (thick)
Private collection
Photo: © Canadian Museum of Civilization, Steven Darby

apron" of Zulu women, a garment that still exists today. They were also used on the fibre belts that indicated a woman's maternity (Figure 10). These belts still exist as well, although they are now decorated with glass beads. It is likely that brass had replaced iron, and in this regard, Berglund remarked that iron, among the Zulus, "stands for productivity in women, animals and fields."[23]

Iron was used in eastern Africa to make bracelets and anklets, beads, and especially necklaces in the form of rings to which chain pendants were added (Figure 11). These necklaces, worn by men and women, were common to many cultures in East Africa.[24] Chains were used in abundance to decorate necklaces, earrings and belts. Some of these ornaments continued to be worn into the early twentieth century, and then disappeared following the arrival of beads. Bracelets and earrings consisting of spirals of iron and brass wire are still worn, particularly by Samburu women, although their use is increasingly rare. Glass bead versions were created to replace them. The *inkalulungani* iron anklets of the married Maasai women are still worn today (Figure 12). The neck rings of iron or copper/brass (*alagama*) worn by married Turkana women, which indicate their husbands' generation,[25] have survived to the present day, as have the *urraur* and *isurutia* brass earrings of Samburu and Maasai women that play an essential role in the lifecycles of both men and women (Figures 13 and 14).

Until recently, the Oromo of Ethiopia continued to wear metal bracelets indicating specific status such as leader, wife or mother of a son (Figure 18). According to Aneesa Kassam, in the Oromo culture, iron, which came from a meteorite, "fell from heaven. In Oromo, there are

Figure 13

Urraur
Earrings
Samburu, Kenya
Second half of the 20th century
Brass
4 cm (l) x 2.2 cm (d)
The Consolata Missionaries, Canada
Photo: © Canadian Museum of Civilization, Steven Darby

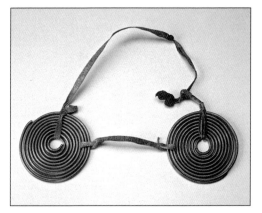

Figure 14

Isurutia
Ornament
Maasai, Kenya
Second half of the 20th century
Brass and animal hide
24 cm (l) x 25.4 cm (w)
Private collection
Photo: © Canadian Museum of Civilization, Steven Darby

vast numbers of ornaments made of iron and its substitutes, copper, brass and more recently, aluminum, which are collectively known as *sibbilla*."[26] She also notes that "When a man marries, his wife receives metal ornaments, bracelets (*meeti*) worn on the left arm and necklaces (*qalim*) … In Oromo, iron is symbolically a 'dead' material, and is an appropriate gift, as marriage itself is seen as a kind of death, in which a husband 'kills' his wife by spilling her virginal blood."[27] It was only after the birth of her first son that she could wear bracelets on her right arm. Again according to Kassam, the right arm represented life, and the woman displayed the birth of her son as a "trophy."[28] She could also sew the brass disk known as *benaac'u* onto the back of her clothing as a sign of maturity and status (Figure 16).

Figure 15 Maasai woman wearing the ornaments of a young wife. Kenya, early 20th century.

Photo: A. C. Hollis. *The Masai: Their Language and Folklore*, 1905.

Among the Turkana of northern Kenya, when a man or a woman died, their ornaments were redistributed to their close relatives, and their iron bracelets given to their children who could suck on them to cure illness.[29] Among the Maasai and the Samburu, a man's metal bracelets were inherited by his sons upon his death.

The use of iron and other metals thus assumed particular significance. This included silver, the metal used most often for jewellery in Ethiopia by Christians and Muslims alike. The availability of a large quantity of silver in Ethiopia can be attributed to the introduction, as early as the eighteenth century, of Austrian thalers (coins) bearing the image of the Empress Maria Theresa. These were melted down by silversmiths to recover the metal. Virtually all of the ornaments that served as the dowries of Somali and Oromo women were, or still are made of silver, and were obtained from silversmiths in urban centres. These jewels enhanced beauty while also serving as capital to help women survive through lean times.[30]

The meaning given to metals has gradually been lost with the growing use of materials that are both literally and figuratively less "heavy." Aluminum, for example, was, and still is used as a substitute for iron and, as such, probably retained iron's significance.[31] In East Africa, it was salvaged from *sufuria* cooking pots, then hammered and used by the Turkana to make the earrings worn by married women and nose ornaments for men (Figure 17). Oromo women wore *qalim* necklaces of aluminum with medallions called *riira*, a reference to the Italian lira introduced during the colonial period.[32] Made by blacksmiths, the *riira* was an aluminum disk

Figure 16 The *benaac'u* recognized the achievement of motherhood of Oromo women.

Benaac'u
Clothing Adornment
Booran Oromo, Ethiopia
Second half of the 20th century
Brass
17.5 cm (diameter)
Anthropology Department, Université de Montréal 61.57
Photo: © Canadian Museum of Civilization, Steven Darby

Figure 17 These earrings identified Turkana women who had given birth.

Akaparaparat
Earrings
Turkana, Kenya
Second half of the 20th century
Aluminum
7.1 cm (l) x 3.8 cm (w)
The Consolata Missionaries, Canada
Photo: © Canadian Museum of Civilization, Steven Darby

Figure 18 Oromo women indicated their status as wives and mothers through their metal ornaments.
Kenya, late 1970s.
Photo: Gerald Cubitt

Figure 19

Ornament

Oromo (Guji?), Ethiopia
Second half of the 20th century
Animal hide, cowries and plant fibre
1.87 cm (l) x 79 cm (w)

Textile Museum of Canada, Toronto T85.0110
Photo: © Canadian Museum of Civilization, Steven Darby

the size of a large coin and often featured a motif such as a simple cross inside a circle. According to Aneesa Kassam, "this design probably represents a crossroad, a universal symbol of the unknown, which (is) full of ritual portent for the Oromo (Figure 18)."[33]

Aluminum, valued for its brightness and light weight, was also used throughout eastern Africa to make numerous pendants and earrings, as well as beads that decorated ornaments and leather clothing. These beads can still be found today on the aprons and skirts of married Turkana women.

From the predominance of white glass beads in many of these cultures' ornaments, it can be deduced that this colour must have been present for a long time, although in a different form. The two elements of animal origin that enabled people to obtain this white colour were ostrich eggs and cowries, the latter apparently invested with the most meaning and more widely used.

The cowrie, which originates in the Indian Ocean, was used throughout Africa as currency or as a sign of status or wealth. Once bartered with Arab merchants from the coast, it was soon available in local shops, and remains so to this day. It was an element of adornment that was relatively costly, and was thus used sparingly. The function most often attributed to the cowrie is that of fertility symbol, primarily because it is found on a large number of feminine objects and ornaments. Such an interpretation excludes some masculine ornaments that also included this type of shellwork. According to Aneesa Kassam, these shells served in earlier times as amulets to aid in fertility and birth, their colour evoking milk, the vital fluid from the child's mother or from livestock.[34] The particular form of the shell, which could evoke the female sexual organs, further reinforces this interpretation. According to Raymond Silverman, the *gorfa* milk containers of the Booran women of Ethiopia (Figure 20) suggested an analogy with the female form by their round shape, the fact that they were filled with milk, and also "by the cowrie shells attached to them, symbolizing, by formal analogy, the vagina."[35]

In contrast, none of the principal users of cowries mentions fertility, but suggest, rather, that cowries provide protection against the evil eye.[36] The cowrie was thus placed on objects symbolizing the survival of the family, for example milk or food containers, to protect them from evildoers. Cowries were also used on the Somali *xeedho* food basket, which played an essential part in marriage ceremonies and symbolically represented the bride (Figure 21).[37] The cowrie was clearly identified by Haoua Mohamed, our Somali consultant for the exhibition, as being able to ward off the evil eye, particularly when worn by individuals.[38]

The people who needed cowries as additional protection were those such as children who found themselves in a temporarily fragile state and were potential victims of the evil eye. It was thus current practice from the southern Sudan to South Africa, to place a bracelet, anklet

Figure 20

Gorfa
Container
Booran Oromo, Kenya
Second half of the 20th century
Plant fibre and cowries
32.4 cm (h), 20.9 (external diameter)
Museum of Anthropology, University
of British Columbia, Vancouver ca69
Photo: © Canadian Museum of
Civilization, Steven Darby

or necklace of cowries (white beads are a more recent equivalent and played the same role) around the limbs, necks or waists of babies and very young children. For the same reason, cowries were found on the fibre headbands worn by young Maasai initiates. When a cowrie broke, it was a sign that it had confronted the intense gaze of an individual bearing the evil eye.[39] Cowries were also found on the beaded corsets and jackets of young Dinka men and women, where the shells undoubtedly played the same protective role, as Zeinab Mokwag and Makueng Maliet, contributors to the Dinka section of the **Beads of Life** exhibition, suggested when asked about the uses of the cowrie.[40] This is no doubt also true of the *elelal*, a Booran skin ornament heavily decorated with cowries that was suspended on the wall of the house behind a couple's bed (Figure 22). Also worth noting are the traditional Amhara baby carriers that were decorated with cowries, as were the capes and belts of young married Hamar women of southern Ethiopia. Among the Turkana, it seems that only married women

Figure 21

Xeedho
Wedding Basket
Somali, Ethiopia
Second half of the 20th century
Animal hide, glass beads, cowries,
plant fibre and dyes
31 cm (h), 28 cm (d)

Anthropology Department, Université
de Montréal 61.221
Photo: © Canadian Museum of
Civilization, Steven Darby

Figure 23 Nura Kote, a Borana elder, wears *elelals* during celebrations commemorating his son's birth. Kenya, 1980s.

Photo: Aneesa Kassam

Figure 22

Elelal
Ornamental Skin
Booran Oromo, Ethiopia
Second half of the 20th century
Animal hide, cowries and plant fibre
139 cm (l) x 38.8 cm (w)

Anthropology Department, Université de Montréal 61.53
Photo: © Canadian Museum of Civilization, Steven Darby

were allowed to wear cowries in their finery, in contrast to the ostrich egg beads worn by young girls.

In East Africa, a large number of the ornaments worn by pregnant women contained cowries. According to Aneesa Kassam, this shell could represent the relationship between mother and child, especially a son, since it could be found during many of the occasions associated with male offspring. Among the Gabbra (Oromo) of northern Kenya, for example, when a mother gave birth to a son, she made him two bracelets and two anklets, each consisting of four cowries (*elela*) hanging from strips of leather. When the baby was weaned, the mother sewed these sixteen cowries onto her leather belt, thus indicating that she had given birth to a healthy son.[41] Kalenjin mothers in Kenya also wore this type of belt. It appears that these belts had multiple functions. They showed that a woman had given birth to a child, either a son or a firstborn, and that the child had survived the precarious first months of life. They also ensured protection of the child and its mother until the child reached a certain stage of independence such as being weaned or being able to walk. Often, the same cowries that served to protect the child were later transferred to other objects such as his milk gourd, or used on his ornaments during his initiation, thus reinforcing his protection.

While it is true that the cowrie is used less often by men, in some regions such as southern Ethiopia, notably among the Booran and the Konso, the cowrie was used equally by men and

Figure 24

Nkata
Head Ornament
Tonga, Zambia
Second half of the 20th century
Cowries and plant fibre
10.7 cm (diameter)
Glenbow Museum, Calgary R383.8
Photo: © Canadian Museum of Civilization, Steven Darby

Figure 25 Among the Tonga, all young female initiates were required to wear the *nkata* ring, which was sewn into their hair. Zimbabwe, 1956.
Photo: Darrel Plowes, AfriPix

women. It was also seen among certain peoples of eastern Africa, especially in some of the headdresses of mature Luo men. In southern Africa, cowries were much less prevalent. Was it more difficult for the shells to reach these regions? It is worth noting however, that ornaments such as the *nkata* (Figure 24), which was composed of cowries placed in a circlet and sewn with braided fibre, were worn on top of the head by Tonga girls of Zimbabwe following their initiation (Figure 25). Another example is the cowrie headband, *ingqoqo*, worn in earlier times on specific ritual occasions by Xhosa girls, brides, young women and men. Xhosa babies sometimes wore a belt that included a number of cowries on which they could cut their teeth,

Figure 26 The beads of ostrich eggshell that adorned the *arach* could have protected the fertility of young Turkana girls.

Arach
Apron
Turkana, Kenya
Second half of the 20th century
Goatskin or sheepskin, ostrich eggshell, glass beads and plant fibre
28 cm (l) x 25.5 cm (w)
Provincial Museum of Alberta, Edmonton H96.55.46
Photo: © Canadian Museum of Civilization, Steven Darby

Figure 27

Apron
San, Botswana
Second half of the 20th century
Animal hide, ostrich eggshell, plant fibre and plastic button
32.8 cm (l) x 33.9 cm (w)
Photo: © Canadian Museum of Civilization, CMC-B-III-135, Steven Darby, T2004-278

although the primary role of these necklaces was undoubtedly a protective one.[42] Could the white beads and buttons used in great quantities on the adornments of the Ndebele, Zulu, Xhosa, etc. as well as in the ritual hairstyles and costumes of diviners indicate that cowries were originally used?

Another shell used in large quantities was the *conus* shell, known as *ndoro* or *mpande* in Zambia and Zimbabwe. When cut, the base of this conical shell formed a white disk that Ila men of Zambia placed on their foreheads as a sign of status. It was also worn around the neck by married women among the Tonga and other peoples. According to Bibiana Nalwiindi Seaborn, a contributor to the Tonga section of the **Beads of Life** exhibition, the *mpande* had a protective and even healing power.[43] Young men in East Africa used these white disks during their period of initiation, and during the nineteenth century they were commonly integrated into necklaces. Later, they were replaced by plastic buttons, and in Zimbabwe by porcelain imitations.

Figure 28 Traditional method for making beads of ostrich eggshell. San, Botswana, 2003.

Photo: Paul Wellhauser, Nharo!

The original function of these objects has been lost. While their use in inducing fertility must be questioned since it is not clearly articulated by the people who used them, there is repeated mention of the function of protection against evil influences for those who bore within them the future of the entire group, i.e. young pubescent girls, pregnant women, mothers and children.

It is possible that beads of ostrich shell found on ornaments in East Africa have played a similar protective role. They are still seen today on protective charms for children, and on the *arach* apron of young Turkana girls (Figure 26). In earlier times, they were also found on a number of belts and ornaments worn by Turkana women.[44] The Turkana women of certain clans wore a necklace of ostrich egg beads for each child, and blessed the beads with water while thinking of their offspring.[45] Throughout East Africa, ostrich egg beads were sewn flat onto leather backings or threaded together to make necklaces. They have almost entirely disappeared from use. This was also one of the essential components of adornment among the San of Botswana before they adopted glass beads (Figure 27). The protection of wild animals in Africa has contributed to the abandonment of beads

Figure 29 Amber is known throughout the Horn of Africa for its medicinal properties.

Unabi
Necklace
Somali, Ethiopia
Second half of the 20th century
Silver and amber or copal
29 cm (diameter) x 4 cm (thick)
Anthropology Department, Université de Montréal 61.265
Photo: © Canadian Museum of Civilization, Steven Darby

made of ostrich egg. Today, the ostrich eggs used by the settled San for tourist objects come from breeding farms.[46]

Other materials with medicinal properties are still worn today. In Ethiopia, these include amber, or copal,[47] its substitute. Both are found in the necklaces of Oromo and Somali women, as well as in prayer necklaces. They have long been ascribed supernatural and healing powers.[48] Upon her marriage, a Somali woman received long necklaces of amber as a form of security (Figure 29).[49]

Ivory and horn were also used to make charms, and certainly played a significant role in the protection of the individual. They were also used in the creation of delicately sculpted ornaments (Figure 30). Ivory bracelets worn by men in both eastern and southern Africa were a sign of status (Figure 31). The Samburu used ivory to make earrings for young people, or charms designed to protect the lives of children (Figure 32).

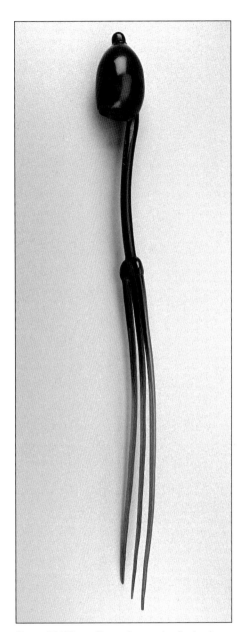

Figure 30 This snuff container made of animal horn is also a comb.

Snuff Container

Zulu?, South Africa

Late 19th or early 20th century

Horn

Snuff container: 3.5 cm (h) x 4.6 cm (w); entire ornament: 40.8 cm (l)

Redpath Museum, Montreal 04247

Photo: © Canadian Museum of Civilization, Steven Darby

The clothing of men and women in eastern and southern Africa has changed radically over the past century. Two essential materials, leather from the skins of wild and domestic animals and plant fibres, were once used to make this clothing. Leather was a material endowed with great importance. Today, traditional skin garments are still used in rites and ceremonies. As we shall see in greater detail in Chapter 5, female skin skirts were predominant in eastern and southern Africa, and indicated the status of the married woman. They included the *buong* of the Dinka, the *abuo* of the Turkana, the *olokesana* of the Maasai, the Iraqw skirt made during the *marmo* ritual, the *isidwaba* of the Zulu, and the *isikhaka* of the Xhosa. These skirts were decorated with beads (metal and cowries in earlier times, glass today) and were composed of several skins (cow, goat or sheep, etc.) sewn together.

Animals that had been carefully chosen for their health, gender and colour were sacrificed on specific occasions rather than on a daily basis. Their meat was distributed to men and women, young and old, according to precise rules. The skin was then dried, softened and smeared with grease and ochre by the women. Skins were used not only as garments, but also as mats to sit on, to wrap specific ritual objects, and in certain regions to smother the sacrificial ox during birth rituals, initiations, marriages, blessing ceremonies and mourning. According to accounts gathered by Anthony Barrett, among the Turkana, the ritualization of the fabrication and use of the *adwel*[50] marriage apron (Figure 33) was highly complex. Depending on the woman's clan, several types of skins could be used. These were provided by the family of her future husband and could include black or white goats (ram or doe), gazelle and sheep, etc., the colour and gender of the animal being equally important. However, other factors sometimes had to be considered. In certain clans, women were not allowed to wear aprons made from the skins of animals without

Figure 31

Photo: © Canadian Museum of Civilization, Steven Darby

Left:	*Centre:*	*Right:*
Arm Ornament	**Bracelet**	***Umxhaka***
Shilluk or Nuer, Sudan	Konso, Ethiopia	**Bracelet**
Late 19th or early 20th century	Second half of the 20th century	Xhosa, South Africa
Ivory	Ivory and aluminum	Late 19th or early 20th century
19.4 cm (l) x 13.5 cm (w) x 7.4 cm	0.72 cm (thick), 11.9 cm (external	Ivory and lead
(high)	diameter)	3.4 cm (h), 13.4 cm (d)
Redpath Museum, Montreal 03986	Anthropology Department, Université de	CMC-B-III-9
	Montréal 61.191	

Figure 32 *Left ring:* a piece of wood, obsidian, a fragment of animal hide and a fragrant protective root. *Right ring:* two pieces of carved ivory.

Lchani
Charms
Samburu, Kenya
Second half of the 20th century
Iron, glass beads, wood, root, obsidian, animal hide and ivory
Each: 10 cm (l)

Anthropology Museum, University of Winnipeg E2A-109 & E2A-13
Photo: © Canadian Museum of Civilization, Steven Darby

horns while their husbands were alive. Ignoring this taboo would bring misfortune to the couple. Important taboos were often related to the use of these marriage aprons. On the wedding day, the skin apron fulfilled several ritual functions meant to show the symbolic entry of the woman into the village, and thus into the family and clan of her husband. In addition, the shirts could not be allowed to get wet until the birth of the couple's first child. If this should happen, a purification ritual had to be held. It was thought that if this ritual was not performed, the woman would remain sterile or her children would die.[51]

The *isidwaba*, a large, impressive skirt of leather blackened with charcoal and worn by Zulu women, has all but disappeared. It has been replaced today with a fabric skirt. Since a family's livestock was considered to be the property of the ancestors, these skirts "stood for the presence of the living dead and the entire male ancestry."[52] Their protective power for mothers or future mothers is thus obvious.

Leather was used not only for clothing but also for important ornaments such as the bands of skin worn in the earlobes of initiated women in East Africa, the belts of married women, and for various other functions. In the Oromo culture, for example, certain wise men of high rank were recognized by their *medic'c'a* bracelets. An animal was specially sacrificed for the occasion and its skin cut into strips and worn around the wrist by high-ranking dignitaries and their men.[53] Other members of the society wore similar bracelets derived from a sacrifice, and all Maasai and Samburu participants of an important ceremony wore similar rings (*ilkerreti*) as a form of blessing.

Among the Xhosa, the *ubulunga* necklace made from the hairs of a specific cow's tail (Figure 34) was a prayer to the ancestors requesting their protection against evil while also

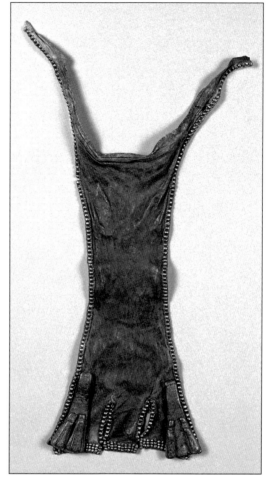

Figure 33 The *adwel* decorated with metal beads was reserved for mothers. It assumed an important symbolic function in daily life and during ceremonies related to birth, marriage and mourning.

Adwel
Apron
Turkana, Kenya
Second half of the 20th century
Goatskin or sheepskin, iron, copper and plant fibre
59.5 cm (l) x 54.3 cm (w)

On loan from the William and Barbara McCann Collection
Photo: © Canadian Museum of Civilization, Steven Darby

ensuring wisdom and good health. The household's eldest son inherited this cow, which was called the "cow of the necklace." The cow could not be killed under any circumstances, or given away in payment of a debt.[54]

Animal skins were an important part of the ritual cycle since they were obtained during specific sacrifices and subsequently reused under important circumstances in people's lives. They supported these individuals by conferring the animal's blessing upon them.

Figure 34 This necklace was worn to honour the ancestors.

Ubulunga
Necklace
Xhosa, South Africa
Late 19th or early 20th century
Glass beads, cow hair, animal hide, glass button and sinew
33.7 cm (l) x 13.5 cm (w)
Provincial Museum of Alberta, Edmonton H64.6.107
Photo: © Canadian Museum of Civilization, Steven Darby

The hides and parts of such animals as leopards, monkeys, gnus and lions were also used to make clothing, ornaments and personal objects. Both in eastern and southern Africa, these items were worn primarily by men. These served as symbols of a mature man's status, of dignitaries within the Zulu kingdom, or even as decorative elements in the adornments of young initiates. The choice of animal was carefully considered as it would convey information about the wearer.

Bird feathers played a major role in personal adornment. Among the Samburu and other peoples of the region, the feathers of certain birds were assigned to specific age groups and genders. These designations were often derived from origin myths in which wild animals played a role. For instance, the names of birds were used in songs sung by young people as a means of indicating the characters of others (by analogy). The feather "pompoms" placed on the tops of the spears and shields of the Acholi, Turkana and Samburu were often signs of peace. In addition, the hairstyles of Turkana men included black or white ostrich feathers to indicate status. The famous parade headdress of the Maasai *morans* (initiates) worn in dances and important ceremonies was made entirely of ostrich feathers sewn on a leather frame (Figure 35).

Plant fibres were part of the composition of many of the fringed skirts and aprons worn by young women from Sudan to the Cape, as well as of many ornaments, particularly in southern Africa. It is likely that many beaded Zulu ornaments were once made of this material. In East Africa, plant fibre was part of the composition of ceremonial ornaments, including the initiation headband of the young Maasai and Samburu (the *olmarisian* and *sirimini* respectively). The necklace of Pokot girls announcing their upcoming initiation was made of stems of wild asparagus (Figure 36). Plant fibre, often sisal, was widely used as beading thread. It was also one of the principal components of the *mporro* marriage necklace, which was made of palm fibre and worn by Samburu and Rendille women (Figure 37).

Farther to the north, plant fibre was one of the principal components of the Oromo milk container, the *gorfa*, a woven basket that had important symbolic functions (Figure 21). These containers were also part of various ceremonies such as the "name-giving" for a firstborn male during which they were exhibited by all women participants as proof of the family's prosperity.[55] In other ceremonies, gifts of milk were made with the help of the *gorfa*.[56] According to Raymond Silverman, several ritual activities involving braiding, particularly braiding of the hair among the Borana (Oromo), could indicate that "weaving in Borana (Oromo) is associated with fertility."[57] (Figure 38)

Along with many Bantu peoples of southern Africa, the Zulu have a long tradition of grass weaving. Woven grasses were used for baskets, as well as mats for sleeping, sitting and eating. *Incema* grass was used for special women's belts worn after the birth of a first child and for belts worn by young people. According to Carol Boram-Hays, mats linked to sleep would have had symbolic associations with the ancestors because they sometimes communicated with the living through dreams. According also to Sandra Klopper, natural fibres are often associated with the notion of fertility.[58] They were widely used in southern Africa to make the clothing elements of young initiates. Again according to Boram-Hays, it is possible that the *incema* grass in these objects enabled the wearers to enter into a relationship with their ancestors

Figure 35 The feathers of certain birds indicated a particular status. This headdress was worn by Maasai *morans* during the *Eunoto* ceremony.

Esidai
Headdress
Maasai, Kenya
Second half of the 20th century
Ostrich feathers, plant fibre, glass beads and animal hide
53 cm (l) x 45 cm (w) (including feathers)
University of Alberta Art and Artifact Collection
Museums and Collections Services, Edmonton 983.57.1.15
Photo: © Canadian Museum of Civilization, Steven Darby

as a means of promoting reproductive capabilities.[59] Zulu women have transferred their knowledge of basket-weaving to the making of beaded ornaments, keeping not only the same braiding and weaving techniques, but also the same contrasting patterns.

People wore charms made of plant material to protect themselves against illnesses and misfortune. In East Africa, the charms often took the form of small leather bags containing a plant-based powder prepared by the medicine man. These charms were visible around the necks of their wearers and communicated a part of their personal history. Some Samburu charms were made of wood, while others were made of fragrant roots, which were grated, placed on the tongue, chewed, and then spit out to summon divine protection (see figure 32). Xhosa women wore necklaces bearing medicinal roots, enabling them to care for a sick child.

Figure 36 Young Pokot girls wore this necklace in anticipation of their upcoming initiation. Kenya, 1990s.
Photo: Adrian Warren (www.lastrefuge.co.uk)

A final significant element in ornamentation was colour. Pigments were obtained from natural materials, minerals, plants, etc. and used in myriad ways. Colour will be discussed in detail in the next chapter.

In earlier days, many of the components of the traditional dress of eastern and southern African people were endowed with essential significance for their users. Ornaments and clothing were only a small part of a range of objects and materials of natural origin that were used in ritual activities on a daily basis, as well as during ceremonies, for the protection of people, livestock, and goods.

As the natural materials disappeared from use, new materials imported from the West such as glass beads and cotton fabrics took their place, and temporarily preserved the meanings the original materials conveyed.

Figure 37 The *mporro* is rapidly disappearing. Samburu women today prefer to wear Maasai-style beaded necklaces that are lighter and more brightly coloured.

Mporro
Necklace
Samburu, Kenya
Second half of the 20th century
Fabric, palm fibres, red ochre, iron and glass beads
27.4 cm x 22 cm x 12.5 cm
Photo: © Canadian Museum of Civilization, CMC-2003.197.1, Steven Darby, T2004-279

Figure 38 Booran women spent months braiding the *gorfa*, which they used to carry and preserve milk from their cows. Ethiopia, 1993.

Photo: Neal Sobania and Raymond Silverman

Endnotes

1. See Chapter 4.
2. V.L. Webb, "Fact and Fiction: Nineteenth-Century Photographs of the Zulu," *African Arts*, 25(1), UCLA, 1992.
3. Marie-Louise Labelle: Information gathered during fieldwork among the Maasai, 1984–1985.
4. Marie-Louise Labelle, "*Le Guerrier Maasai, histoire d'un mythe, récit d'une rencontre*," Doctoral thesis in Anthropology and Social Sciences, EHESS, 1996.
5. Aneesa Kassam, Introduction to the Oromo section of "Traditional Ornament," unpublished exhibition catalogue, National Museums of Kenya (Nairobi), 1985.
6. Francis Mading Deng, *The Dinka and Their Songs* (Oxford: Clarendon Press, 1973).
7. Ibid., p. 16.
8. Erich Heinrich Bigalke, *Dress, Personal Decoration and Ornament Among the Ndlambe, Annals of the Cape Provincial Museums* (Natural History), 9(4): 65-90, 1972, p. 71.
9. The young bride must not utter a single word that might have a sound similar to the name of one of the members of her husband's family. In principle, this means that each word in her vocabulary must have a substitute. Dawn Costello reminds us that Xhosa women went in groups to shop for beads in order to avoid having to utter the name of a colour description that might sound like the name of their mother-in-law or father-in-law, or any other senior member of their husband's family. Dawn Costello, *Not Only for Its Beauty: Beadwork and Its Cultural Significance Among the Xhosa-Speaking Peoples* (Pretoria: University of South Africa, 1990).
10. Carol S. Boram-Hays, "A History of Zulu Beadwork 1890-1997: Its Types, Forms and Functions," M.A. dissertation, Ohio State University, 2000.
11. Ibid.
12. These "reminders" of the deceased could be a few beads concealed under a necklace, or an iron bracelet, a tobacco box, a headrest, etc.
13. Anthony J. Barrett, *Turkana Iconography: Desert Nomads and Their Symbols* (Kijabe Printing Press, 1998).
14. See Chapter 4.
15. See Chapter 5.
16. See Chapter 5.
17. Catherine Vanderhaeghe, *Les bijoux d'Éthiopie : Les centres d'orfèvrerie de 1840 à la fin du XXème siècle*, Doctoral thesis in Archaeology and Art History, *Université catholique de Louvain, Faculté de Philosophie et Lettres, Institut Supérieur d'Archéologie et d'Histoire de l'Art*, December 2001.
18. Aneesa Kassam, "Iron and Beads: Male and Female Symbols of Creation. A Study of Ornament Among Booran Oromo," in Hooder, I., ed., *The Meaning of Things: Material Culture and Symbolic Expression* (London: Unwin Hyman, 1989), pp. 23–32.
19. Deng, 1973.
20. T. Maggs, 1992, "My Father's hammer never ceased its song day and night: The Zulu ferrous metalworking industry," Natal Museum Journal of Humanities, 4:67-87, quoted by Frans Roodt, *Zulu MetalWorking*, in Wood, Marilee et al., *Zulu Treasures of Kings & Commoners: A Celebration of the Material Culture of the Zulu People* (The Local History Museums, 1996).
21. Labelle, 1996.
22. C. G. Kennedy, "Prestige Ornaments: The Use of Brass in the Zulu Kingdom," *African Arts*, vol. 24(3) (Los Angeles: UCLA, 1991).
23. Axel-Ivar Berglund, *Zulu Thought-Patterns and Symbolism* (Indiana University Press, 1989).
24. One of the ornaments of this type that still exists today can be found in the shape of a necklace worn by the Hamar women of Ethiopia.

25. As well as the fact that the dowry had been fully paid. Günter Best, *Marakwet and Turkana: New Perspectives on the Material Culture of East African Societies* (Museum für Völkerkunde, 1993).

26. Kassam, 1989, pp. 25–6.

27. Ibid., p. 29.

28. Ibid., 1989.

29. Barrett, 1998.

30. Vanderhaeghe, 2001.

31. Kassam, 1985.

32. Paolo Tablino, *The Gabra Camel Nomads of Northern Kenya* (Paulines Publications Africa, 1999).

33. Kassam, 1985.

34. Ibid.

35. Raymond Silverman, ed., *Ethiopia: Traditions of Creativity*, Michigan State University Museum (University of Washington Press, 1999), p. 76.

36. Haoua Mohammed, Research Assistant/Consultant for **Beads of Life**, Somali culture, translated by Asma Jamaa, interviewed on April 7, 2003 at the Canadian Museum of Civilization.

37. Somali women wrapped and decorated the *xeedho*, and encircled it with complicated knots. On the seventh day of the marriage ceremonies, the groom and his companions had to open it in a particular order. The reputation of the groom depended upon their patience and success. The food contained in the basket was then distributed to the guests. Information gathered from Haoua Mohammed.

38. Haoua Mohammed: "It is used to chase away the evil eye, for children it is placed on their ankles, for girls in the hair, and girls also wear it as a pendant around their neck; it removes the evil eye."

39. Labelle, 1996.

40. Interview with Zeinab Mokwag and Makueng Maliet, Research Assistants/Consultants for the **Beads of Life** exhibition, Dinka culture, interviewed on April 4, 2003 at the Canadian Museum of Civilization: "Sometimes you can wear them for decoration but the meaning of this is to protect. Decoration and protection. The shell can break if it meets someone with bad eye. When I was younger, my grandfather, if they see somebody who had a bad eye, he said come, come and bring me the *gak*! The people can throw them up, they are like magicians, they can read by using the shells. They count them, and if the bottom is down or up, it has meanings."

41. Tablino, 1999.

42. Bigalke, 1972.

43. Bibiana Nalwiindi Seaborn, Research Assistant/Consultant for **Beads of Life**, Tonga culture, interviewed on October 23, 2003 at the Canadian Museum of Civilization.

44. Although they were cowrie users, in most instances the Turkana used ostrich eggs that were available locally and to which they attributed the same protective properties.

45. Barrett, 1998.

46. See Chapter 6.

47. Vanderhaeghe: "Although fossilized amber was the object of intense commerce in Europe and North Africa, it seems more reasonable, in the absence of chemical analysis, to consider that the amber material used in Ethiopian jewellery was rather copal, a natural resin which existed in a semi-fossilized state. It is found in quantity on the island of Zanzibar from which it was exported to Arabia and the eastern coasts of Africa."

48. Ibid.: "The Romans used it as an amulet or as a medicine for sore throats, grains of amber being brought in this case in a necklace tightened around the neck. Its curative powers are still recognized today in Europe, where amber is used in homeopathic remedies."

49. Ibid.: "Amber embellishes the jewellery of Muslims of the coastal regions and Harar. Traded since neolithic times, amber has always been deeply appreciated for its curative and prophylactic powers,

which have made it valued for use primarily as a magical stone or amulet. I have noted besides that most of the jewellery made of amber is associated with silver talismanic cases."

50. *Akodat* (or *esiya*) designates the wedding apron, often decorated with glass beads. The *adwel*, decorated with metal beads, is worn only following the birth of the first child. The *adwel* is thus used here as a generic term for reasons of simplification. For more detail on their differences, see Chapter 5.

51. Barrett, 1998.

52. The author is using the word "shield" to describe this skirt. Robert Papini, "Some Zulu Uses for the Animal Domains: Livestock (imfuyo) and Game (izinyamazane)" in Wood, Marilee et al., *Zulu Treasures of Kings & Commoners: A Celebration of the Material Culture of the Zulu People*, p. 185.

53. Kassam, 1989.

54. Bigalke, 1972.

55. Silverman, 1999: "During the naming ceremony for a firstborn male infant, *gubbisa*, each participating married woman brings a *gorfa* filled with milk or curdled milk, and hangs it in the celebrating household. More than one hundred *gorfas* are hung. The *gorfas* are brought to feed the guests, who continue to sing/chant well into the night. A piece of meat from the sacrificial animal is attached to each *gorfa* and each woman brings the meat back home."

56. Ibid., 1999.

57. Ibid., p. 75.

58. Sandra Klopper, "The Art of Zulu-Speakers in Northern Natal-Zululand," quoted in Carol Boram-Hays, 2000.

59. Boram-Hays, 2000.

GLASS BEADS AND COLOUR INTERPRETATION

3

"Where did the beads come from?"[1] This question is frequently asked by those who have used beads since their arrival in Africa. A kind of mystery surrounds glass beads, no doubt linked to the extraordinary and sometimes dramatic circumstances under which they arrived in eastern and southern Africa long ago. According to certain myths, this "divine" material accompanied the appearance on earth of key figures or important clans; according to other legends it literally fell from the sky. The Maasai, for example, believed that the first diviner and prophet (*oloiboni*) descended from the sky along a string of beads.

When glass beads brought by Europeans arrived in massive quantities in southern Africa and subsequently in eastern Africa, they were an immediate success. Such beads were not unknown in Africa, however, since they had been made in ancient Egypt, especially in Alexandria. Furthermore, beads from India in particular, but also from Iran and the Middle East, had been transported to the African continent at least as early as the ninth century A.D., brought from the shores of the Indian Ocean at Lamu, Mombasa, Zanzibar and Delagoa Bay by caravans of Arab merchants seeking ivory and slaves. The Maasai named the compass point East, *oloosaen*, "it of the beads," because that was the direction from which beads arrived in earlier times. These early beads were irregular in size and were used very sparingly in ornaments. Their colours and quantities were limited. In addition, it is likely that the peoples living close to the coasts and trading directly with Arab merchants initially had a monopoly on glass beads, which were later traded in a more limited fashion with the peoples of the interior.[2] With the exploration and subsequent colonization of eastern and southern Africa, this situation changed radically. European explorers following the trail of the Arab caravans brought along great quantities of beads, offering them in exchange for rights of passage through the remote lands of the interior. In doing so, they also created a demand. Early European beads came primarily from Venice and Murano, a monopoly that was broken during the twentieth century by Jablonek in Bohemia (today's Czech Republic), which then became the principal supplier of glass beads to Africa for most of the twentieth century. Portuguese, Dutch and English colonists each assumed control of this lucrative trade in their turn.

The new European-made beads were more uniform in size, and their well-defined and brilliant colours contrasted sharply with those of older beads. The widespread use of these new beads coincided with a historical moment in southern and eastern Africa, namely, the advent of European colonization. Traditional economic systems were overturned as societies adopted a market economy; the beads had to be purchased, often at great expense, in local shops that also sold cotton fabrics, sugar, flour, tea and many other types of merchandise. Little by little, instead of serving as mere decorative colour elements in adornments made of local materials, European beads replaced traditional materials to become the actual "fabric" of the ornament, and even occasionally of the garment itself. Thus, the iron necklaces of the Maasai became necklaces of beads threaded onto commercial iron wire. The fibre skirts of young Zulu and

Xhosa girls became fringes of beads, and cotton skirts embroidered with beads replaced women's traditional skin skirts.

The result was a veritable revolution in personal adornment, thanks to the ingenuity of the women. Some utilized their basket-weaving skills in working with beads, while others developed new techniques to accommodate this new material. European beads were appreciated for their solidity, the quality and variety of their colours and above all, their brilliance. In order to acquire beads, people would sell some of their livestock, which in turn reduced the availability of the skins that had once been used extensively for clothing. But skin clothing itself would soon be abandoned in favour of the cotton fabrics that were flooding the market.

The widespread adoption of beads followed on the heels of the European invasion of Africa, during which settlers annexed the best lands. The peoples who lived on these fertile lands suffered the most from this invasion. The upheaval in their traditional way of life led to modifications in their traditional dress, often resulting in a permanent and sometimes forced abandonment of traditional clothing and ornaments. Most of the nomadic pastoral peoples

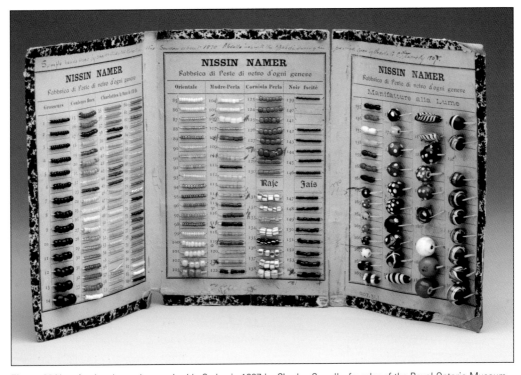

Figure 39 Venetian bead sampler acquired in Sudan in 1907 by Charles Currelly, founder of the Royal Ontario Museum.

Trade beads sample panel
Sudan
Late 19th century
Cardboard, glass beads and thread
40.5 cm (l) x 20.5 cm (w)
Royal Ontario Museum, Toronto HI 100 (907.31.1)
With the permission of the Royal Ontario Museum © ROM

living on semi-arid savannah were less affected by Western influence. For these peoples, traditional dress survives to this day, as can be seen among certain peoples of southern Ethiopia and northern Kenya.

Between the arrival of European glass beads in southern Africa and their arrival in eastern Africa, there is a historical time lag that relates to the different stages of colonization in each region. In South Africa, European beads arrived in vast quantities at the beginning of the nineteenth century, and, among the Zulu, were at first reserved for the elite, since the Zulu kings controlled their trade. However, with increasing numbers of Europeans arriving in the region, bringing with them great quantities of these precious beads, and with the dismantling of the Zulu kingdom during the Anglo-Zulu War in 1879, access to beads became more general, encouraging a flourishing of regional styles. In East Africa, however, extensive use of European beads dates more often from the beginning of the twentieth century. This date coincides with the end of European exploration and the beginning of systematic colonization within this region. This difference persists today. Several East African peoples still use traditional beaded ornaments on a daily basis, whereas in southern Africa, their use is mostly restricted to ceremonies.

European colonists, for whom beadwork was traditionally an "inoffensive" and "respectable" feminine craft, no doubt observed the activity of beading with a benevolent eye. In European countries, beading was an activity practiced by girls and women in polite society and like other needlework, undoubtedly helped to keep them quiet and confined to the hearth. Makueng Maliet, one of the consultants for **Beads of Life**, notes that "it was perhaps a form of colonialism to occupy people with beading in such a way that they wouldn't have time to think about more serious matters."[3] It was from this angle that European colonists, particularly missionaries, would continue to consider this activity, thus affirming to the present day the notion that beading is an essentially decorative and recreational craft with neither social scope nor any real artistic importance. The fact that this activity was strictly feminine further reinforced this idea.

For those who used beads, however, it was nothing of the sort. Glass beads were only a material for the expression of significant aspects of social identity, as seeds had been, or cowrie shells, ostrich eggs, metal beads, and later, plastic buttons and all other materials "recycled" from Western culture. Although the historical and economic implications of the widespread adoption of imported beads were real and without precedent in the history of the peoples of eastern and southern Africa, this adoption did not immediately challenge the uses and functions of traditional dress. Beading was not adopted as a hobby craft, but rather as an effective means of communication, which, as we shall see later, in many cases even favoured an affirmation of identity in the face of foreign invasion. European beads became part of a well-established system of visual communication, not as mere decorative elements, but as active agents of this system, taking up directly where earlier materials had left off.

European beads soon became accessible to all in a range of colours previously unknown in Africa. At certain periods, new sizes, shapes and colours would appear in local shops. These were either adopted or rejected. Colour preferences were precise, and often influenced the commercial decisions of producers and distributors of beads in Africa. While certain novelties managed to pass the test, others were rejected as not fulfilling very specific needs. The tastes of Zulu kings regarding the colours and shapes of beads were known by merchants, and honoured. Many European explorers and colonists must have been disappointed when they brought in certain beads at great cost, only to discover that these were not marketable because they did not correspond to the preferences then in vogue.[4]

The arrival of new colours, sizes and shapes on the local market sometimes produced lively reactions among women. A Maasai woman recounted how she begged her husband to give her the money necessary to buy the brand-new *entepei* bead, a large flat bead that appeared during the 1960s in Kenya, and rapidly became an indispensable decorative element in all adornment.[5] During the final years of British rule, administrators tried to force the young Samburu initiated men (*morans*) to work. Alas, the latter thought of nothing but courting young girls who decked themselves out in necklaces of large red *somi* beads. In order to achieve their purpose, the British could find no solution other than to prevent the trade in these beads. However, their efforts were in vain, as the beads were quickly replaced by others.[6] Sandra Klopper notes that among the Zulu, beads had to be bought by the father of a future bride but adds that it is known that women sought salaried work for the sole purpose of buying beads for their finery and that of their husbands.[7]

Throughout the twentieth century, both in southern and eastern Africa, there was a constant increase in the range of colours. While the trend, in South Africa until the late nineteenth century, and in East Africa until about the mid-twentieth century, was to work with two, three or four colours to create simple contrasts, the availability of new colours permitted the creation of increasingly complex colour combinations and designs. This process continues today.

One of the typical Western preoccupations, despite repeated admonitions from bead users, is to look for the "symbolic" meaning in the use of certain colours, combinations and designs. Ironically, it is when commercial beadwork is becoming widely available that systematic research on the possible "meanings" of beadwork increases. Such symbolic "meanings" even became selling points for merchants who would reveal to a potential buyer the "secret" meaning of any hastily made piece of beadwork being sold. This tendency is not limited to tourist outlets at animal parks in Kenya and southern Africa. It pervades the entire discussion of African beadwork, be it in the media or sometimes even in the scientific literature.

There is not enough space in this book to explore all that has been said about the supposed significance of beadwork in eastern and southern Africa. Instead, we will focus on challenging some of the most common assumptions underlying the supposed symbolism of beads.

The first assumption is that the perception and naming of colours should everywhere be the same and should be based on the Western model. Glass beads users generally found names for artificial colours by borrowing the colour name of the nearest natural element such as a plant, a wild or domesticated animal, etc. This was largely because glass beads had to be integrated within a system in which colours, designs and contrasts had already been named and classified. The naming and classification of colours also corresponded to cultural "priorities" that varied from one region to another and one society to another. As noted by Serge Tornay in *Voir et Nommer les Couleurs* ("Seeing and Naming the Colours"),[8] "the various human cultures, as a function of their natural environment, their way of life and their history, give to colour a variable importance. Few of them, like Western culture, consider colour as a thing in itself, or as a perception removed from other sensorial impressions."[9] Tornay emphasizes the "subjective nature of perception. Our senses give us an image of the world which conforms, not to nature, but to our biological make-up and ... to our cultural heritage."[10] The current error, among those seeking to establish a precise list of the names of colours in a society that is distinct from their own, is therefore to base their research on their own experience of colour. Distracted by a classification system unknown to them, they are often led to believe that the perception of colour among non-Western societies is "inferior to" theirs. Numerous studies, however, have demonstrated the exact opposite.[11]

Bernard Pastoureau takes up this idea in *Blue: The History of a Color*. "Color is, first and foremost a social phenomenon. There is no transcultural truth to color perception, despite what many books based on poorly grasped neurobiology or — even worse — on pseudo-esoteric pop psychology would have us believe." In addition, he states that "It is society that 'makes' color, defines it, gives it its meaning, constructs its codes and values, established its uses, and determines whether it is acceptable or not."[12]

To further complicate matters, again according to Serge Tornay, "few societies, save Western society, consider colour as a thing unto itself or as a perception cut off from other sensory impressions … Colour is not a separate entity."[13]

These corrections are essential since they enable us to realize that hasty attributions of "significance" to the colours of beads, when they are based on a terminology and logic that is purely Western, do not take into account each society's own colour-naming and colour-classification systems.

Thus, for many peoples who practise beadworking in eastern and southern Africa, from the southern Sudan to the Cape, the words for the principal colours are inspired by the coats of animals. Since livestock is so economically and symbolically central to many of these societies, we should take a closer look at this phenomenon.

The list of colours used to describe the coats of animals is nearly infinite, be it among the Dinka, the Oromo, the Turkana, the Samburu, the Maasai or even the Zulu and the Xhosa. The names evoke different nuances of brown, orange, yellow, ochre, grey, black, white, etc. but also patterns,[14] speckled, spotted, striped, streaked, and so on. Among the Dinka, the terms are so precise that they take on a poetic dimension. According to John Ryle, young Dinka men describing their favourite ox reach the heights of "artistic criticism."[15] However, since most Dinka colour terms describe hues of grey, brown or specific configurations of markings, contrasts etc., the difficulty for researchers outside the Dinka culture can prove insurmountable if they try to create a list of colours in the Dinka language to apply them to beads they name blue, red, green, etc. in their own culture.[16] In fact, the words used by the Dinka to name bead colours are the same as those used to designate the colours of livestock. This "difficulty" arose during our discussions with Makueng Maliet and Zeinab Mokwag, who helped us interpret the Dinka ornaments presented in **Beads of Life**. So-called "contradictions" appeared in their naming of colours of the different Dinka beaded corsets. For example, the English term "blue" suddenly became "green."[17] This is because the Dinka word that they used to describe both colours, *ngok*, in fact refers to a kind of grey, and is used for a cow colour. When applied to beads, it can be used indiscriminately to describe both blue and green beads.[18]

Among the Maasai, for whom terminology related to the colours of livestock is equally rich, differences from the Western norm also exist in the naming of bead colours. For example, the same term, *narok*, describes both dark blue and black, as is the case with corresponding Oromo and Turkana terms. By contrast, beads of light blue bear a distinct name: *pus*. Among the Zaramo of Tanzania, "all dark colours (brown, dark blue, grey) are equated with black; light yellow, beige, light grey, or transparent things may be called white; and any color with a reddish tinge can be called red."[19]

Therefore, these divergences in naming and classifying colours and describing patterns should be considered when an attempt is made to interpret the beadwork's possible significations.

The second common assumption is that when beadwork colours and patterns are named after objects, animals or people, they are meant to "represent" or "symbolize" them.

Among the Maasai, as among their neighbours near and far in eastern and southern Africa, most of the colour terms applied to beads describe elements in the immediate environment. The word that describes the dark blue or black colour of a bead is the same as the word used to describe the colour of the sky. The word for a white bead is the same as the word that describes the colour of milk. The word for a green bead is the same as the word that applies to grass. The choice of these terms is of a purely practical nature. The colour analogies by no means justify the interpretations that are still seen at times in scholarly publications: blue in beadwork *is* (or represents) the sky; white *is* milk; green *is* grass; red *is* blood; orange *is* the earth, etc. If these sorts of interpretations were correct, it would mean that a person wearing a Maasai necklace with these colours is seeking to evoke milk, grass, etc. This is patently absurd, since all beaded Maasai ornaments always bear these colours together, and in an equal fashion.

Beyond analogies to colours found in nature, beadwork motifs are also commonly named according to particular patterns in the environment, such as those seen on animals or plants. For example, a coloured pattern found on many Maasai beaded ornaments is named *esinon* after a flower common in Maasailand, but it does not of course represent that flower. The pattern of blue and white beaded stripes found on a popular Maasai beaded necklace is called *enkoitiko*, after both zebra stripes and a striated cloud formation. This in no way means that this necklace evokes or "symbolizes" a zebra or clouds. This pattern is also used to describe a particular cow's coat. Many other terms are used for that purpose, the majority being based on the different configurations of the contrast of white and black. They are an excellent source of terms to describe beadwork patterns.[20]

The question is further complicated in the case of colour naming among peoples of southern Africa such as the Zulus. In the exhibition catalogue *Zulu Treasures*,[21] Marguerite Poland produced a draft inventory of the names of colours of livestock among the Zulu that is consistent with what has just been described for the pastoral peoples of East Africa. Above all, her inventory notes a particular trait, i.e. the description of livestock colours by *analogy* with the names of animals, plants, natural phenomena, etc. Poland sorted the terms by category. For example, many of them are derived from the names of birds. Not only do these terms refer to the colours of birds, but also to their characteristic movements. This produces colour terms such as "the hornbill takes flight," to describe the movement of the bird's white feathers in contrast with its black feathers in flight. The same effect is observed when a cow of this colour walks, exposing the white markings on its legs.[22] Other colours of livestock are named after species of snakes, lizards or other wild animals. At times, different descriptions are combined: a cow has the colour of a bird, but also markings that resemble the silhouette of trees against the sky. Poetic analogies are unlimited. The colours may refer to food such as curdled milk or the appearance of vegetables and fruits when ripe. The weather and the configurations of the land are also an inexhaustible source of words, as are people. There exists, for example, the "beast of the women that cross the river," designating the special configuration of the water when it "covers the legs of women who raise their skirts to cross a stream."[23]

The tendency to use evocative and poetic descriptive terms rather than immutable colour descriptors is also found in the names of bead colours. We will take the colour blue as an example. A review of a mere handful of Zulu terms for the blue proposed by different researchers produces the following results.

The *ijuba* blue is derived from a particular colour of dove, i.e. a lavender shade of blue. Among the Xhosa, light blue is also *ijuba*. But dark blue is *eluhlaza*, which also describes a sort of green.[24] That being said, several types of doves exist, and each of them is of a precise hue: sky blue, or sometimes the dark blue colour of a mountain dove, the grey-blue of a common dove, etc. Certain dark blue beads bear the name of the common ibis, *inkankane*. But the Xhosa tell us that these birds can also be the colour of doves. Of course blue can also be named after the colour of the sky, *isibakabaka*.[25] As for "royal blue," it is derived from the colour of the ocean, *olwandle*. According to certain authors, however, royal blue is instead named after another type of dove called *ihobe*. A certain type of pale blue refers to a young girl, *inkosazana*.[26] The colour *ijoli* is a very dark blue that was used extensively in the colour combinations of the Zulu of the Msinga area.[27] A navy blue, *ufefefe*, also signifies a certain kind of "gossip"[28] and according to the dictionary, refers to a species of blue jay.[29] The terminology continues in this way to infinity, constantly contradicting itself. The same phenomenon occurs for red, green, and every other colour. Considering the range of glass bead colours that have been available in southern Africa from their introduction to the present day, the nomenclature alone can be overwhelming.

However, the problem does not end here. In recent years, beadwork interpretation has been approached as a kind of literary exercise. This leads us to the third assumption commonly made, i.e. that beadwork can be read as a text.

As we have just seen with Maasai beadwork, when a colour is named through analogy with an animal, a natural phenomenon, or even a person, it is tempting to deduce that the colour symbolizes this element, i.e. that the use of this particular colour of bead is deliberately meant to evoke either itself, or the moral characteristics to which it is culturally tied. This idea can be expanded to affirm that when different bead colours are placed together, as for example on a simple necklace, the combination of analogies forms actual structured sentences with poetic content, which in turn form a "message." Some researchers have suggested that the famous "love letters," small necklaces including a central panel of beads that were offered by young girls to their beloved (or vice-versa), contained messages decipherable only by the parties concerned. They suggest that these messages not only indicated a depth of feeling, but also contained information on intent to marry, depending on the way the colour sequences were placed, and sometimes even on the design formed by the beads. Regina Twala[30] proposes several analyses of bead colour sequences as follows:

Green: "Lucky are the cattle that eat in the green pastures passing through the gates of your kraal."

Yellow: "Oh! If I could come and pick those pumpkins from your garden." (A type of yellow is named after the colour of pumpkins.)

Black: "I would then be wearing my black *kaross* [skin skirt]." (Black is the colour of women's skin skirts.)

Red: "Yet my heart is red [sore]."

Yellow: "Because you are poor and have no cattle."[31]

Or:

Yellow: "You are like the excreta of a calf." (This particular kind of yellow is named after the colour of the excrement of a calf, hence the deduction.)

White: "Your purity is full of smudges, spots." (White is intended to mean "purity".)

Red: "Instead of settling down and basking by the fire."

Deep blue: "And be happy as a dove." (Naming through analogy with the blue dove)

Royal blue: "You are as restless and as noisy as the *inkankane* bird." (Refers to the blue of this bird)

Pale yellow: "Therefore one doubts your virginity." (Because this yellow must not be worn by an unmarried girl)

Red: "Appearing several times in the pattern means that the girl delights in kindling fires all over the place."[32]

The possible counter-arguments to this type of interpretation are legion. We will review only a few of the major objections.

No two authors propose the same interpretations for colours and colour combinations. As we have seen, colours sometimes have different names analogous to elements in nature that are themselves changeable, and there are many contradictions between different authors on these names and their references. In addition, the messages being conveyed appear in the form of veritable proverbs or phrases that simply play with colour names, and notably, the multiple elements of the environment from which these are derived. Consequently, they are always different. Under such conditions, how could any single combination of colours on an ornament always imply the same message? How could such a message, if not based on a single definitive code known by all, even be understood by the person to whom it is directed?

The manner in which the syntax of messages is established must also be considered. We are told, for example, that pink placed next to red signifies that one is a lover, but has no economic means. Poverty is said to be evoked by the use of the colour pink. In fact, the word used for "pink" is literally "poor red." If this were true, however, we might question why pink was one of the favourite bead colours of members of the royal court in the time of the Zulu kingdom. Why not also say that this configuration implies a "poor love" or a lack of love? Certain researchers also affirm that such and such a colour, depending on its neighbouring colour, could have positive or negative implications. Who, under such conditions, could possibly decide, not only upon the association of colours with certain moral qualities, ideas or feelings, but also upon their meanings once organized in combinations, and still be perfectly understood by all?

Also, such interpretations do not take into account the enormous changes of fashions (and bead types) that have taken place between the end of the nineteenth century and the present day. Consideration must be given to certain contrasts and designs that were in vogue for a century, but are no longer fashionable, although the basic structure of the ornaments has often remained the same. What is the validity of all of these analyses based on a few examples of ornaments fixed within a given style and period when succeeding and preceding periods are being considered? How should regional variations in style be treated? How do these symbolic codes that are surprisingly precise change through time and space, and according to which criteria?

Moreover, what of practical considerations, such as the time required to make a beaded ornament? How could any message remain valid after several weeks of work? How can a time-consuming work of beading reflect the anecdotal and the temporary?

What of the aesthetic rules that apply to all ornaments of the same period and region? Let us take the example of Zulu beadwork at the end of the nineteenth century, which was highly codified, particularly by the colours and their combinations. Similar colour associations are found, for example, on the neck portion of necklaces with panels, which according to some researchers would contain messages, as on their beaded loops and borders. For example, red is very often underlined with yellow or pink. These choices are visibly of an aesthetic nature. If, as some would like to believe, only certain necklaces include coded messages, what then differentiates them from the ones lacking in meaning, since their aesthetic treatment is the same? Is it not rather, the rhythm, the harmonious contrast of colour associations, the symmetry or lack of symmetry that are essential? Should we not instead analyze the purely aesthetic rules of beadwork, as Frank Jolles has done by distinguishing several colour combinations among the Zulu of Msinga, each of which has a name, without looking for a mysterious symbolic message behind these combinations?[33]

According to Bongani Mthetwa,[34] the basic colour vocabulary is not rigid, but "context-sensitive." In addition, the artist's particular aesthetic and creativity can sometimes obscure the code. Deliberately coded beaded messages are thus made as true puzzles, sometimes taking months to decipher. This would suggest that in general, beadwork was a flexible, evocative medium, capable of holding meaning at certain levels but unlikely to support rigid messages or reward textual analysis.

A Zulu beadworker interviewed by Marilee Wood[35] confirmed that the finished pieces she showed her contained no message. However, she offered to make her a necklace of the *isinyolovane* ("letter") type "as an example of beads that 'speak.'" She then commented on it with perfect ease and in a highly poetic language. Each bead colour seemed to trigger entire sentences, to eventually compose a real story. This could mean that only the maker of a piece of beadwork is able to interpret it, which if true, would considerably reduce its communication potential.

The capacity of beadwork to provide decipherable messages seems to be restricted to "love letters." But Sibongile Nene,[36] who in 2003 interviewed an elder in KwaZulu-Natal about old Zulu beadwork pieces, found that he interpreted different pieces of beadwork in similar ways.[37] In one instance, he interpreted the colours on a beaded belt of the *isigege* type worn by young unmarried women: "Here at the top where it made my heart to be red and then black … she displays spots to say, here a white dot, here a red, one a blue and black, and here she got thin … she says, I have become thin like the blade of grass. This speaks now … all of it speaks. She has thinned like a blade of grass but you will end up taking me in marriage, this says. Here, she is placing patterns of love, the heart … She came through all this line at the top

… but will end up here at the bottom with the black beads in marriage with you … I know that this piece is really talking … beads can really talk. The story can leave you behind … Here she is telling you that she is green here … her heart is green … but she may end up leaving you for another with the black at the bottom."[38]

The same kind of interpretation of beadwork as text emerges from the interviews that Xavier Van der Stappen conducted while in Maasailand. He says "Beads are like letters of the alphabet,[39] their rows represent words, their number defines gender, and their organization announces sentences."[40]

Van der Stappen provides many examples of the interpretation of beadwork as texts. We read for instance, about the successive rows of beads that encircle the handle of a fly whisk: "the row of orange beads represents the father, head of the family … The row of blue beads represents the head of his wife … The six rows of yellow beads symbolize the prosperity of the family … The two rows of beads indicate that the mother has a son who became a Moran."[41] All the colour sequences are read in the same fashion, making statements, evoking animals, people, events, and most of all, mentioning the "peace" that rests with the members of the fly whisk owner's family.

However, this kind of interpretation does not work when we realize that the sequence of beaded rows that is being interpreted here in such a precise way corresponds to standard Maasai aesthetics that have been repeated throughout Maasailand on a vast range of beaded objects for decades. Yellow, which is sometimes put in place of green to form a contrast with red when green beads are lacking, does not, to our knowledge, have a specific meaning attached to it. A row of orange placed next to a row of dark blue beads (here described as representations of the husband and wife) is the usual way Maasai beadworkers associate colours.

Van der Stappen obtains the same kind of comments on the patterns and colours of a Maasai skirt. Beads in particular appear to have been assigned meanings that are in fact blessings aimed at protecting a new bride – the wearer of the skirt on her wedding day. Finally, the chevron patterns that are a distinctive feature of many Maasai beaded skirts are interpreted as follows: they "refer to advice given by the elders: 'Don't expect life to be uniform, it has ups and downs.'"[42] Each beaded object reviewed this way provides lines and lines of texts, most of them being blessings of the kind that Maasai elders provide during ceremonies. The more we progress through them, the less we understand their link with Maasai beadwork colours and patterns.

In debates on the symbolism of beadwork colours, we must question the interaction between the enquirer and the informants. Do informants understand exactly what is being asked of them, especially when we consider linguistic and cultural barriers? Does this quest for meanings correspond to their usual preoccupations and to questions they are used to considering? It is probable that the desire of enquirers to find meanings, as well as the particular form of their questions, are determining factors in the responses they receive. These responses that are designed to satisfy the enquirers are taken at face value, then transformed into precepts applicable to all ornaments. They should instead be considered as a discourse that is not analytical, but corresponds to other forms of communication, like oral poetry, or blessings, as we have seen in the case of the Maasai.

Finally, how can we accept that the need to transmit a coded message (and why should it be coded in the first place?) could or should dominate the aesthetics of beadwork? The two do not proceed from the same intention. One consists literally of writing with the help of beads used as letters, with apparently no concern about the visual impact of their combination. As we have noted earlier, eastern and southern African beadwork follows strict rules when it comes to combining beads. The result is the expression of an ideal order through the mastery of colour contrast, the harmony of patterns, and a search for perfection in the organization of space.

In the next chapter, we will examine a few of the aesthetic rules of beadwork, with the aid of several examples from the Canadian collections.

Endnotes

1. The Zulu king Dingane would have asked: "Where do they come from? What are they made of? How are they made? Cannot we learn to make them?" He would have asked a missionary "whether it would be possible to get a beadmaker to come and live at the royal court." Allen Francis Gardiner, *Narrative of a Journey to the Zoolu Country in South Africa (undertaken in 1835)*, 1836, quoted by Boram-Hays, p. 516. Kuwee Kumsa, of Oromo origin, asked us: "So where did those Oromo get these beads from?" Research Assistant/Consultant for **Beads of Life**, Oromo culture, interviewed on April 25, 2003 at the Canadian Museum of Civilization. Makueng Maliet, of Dinka origin and living in Ottawa, asked us the same question: "Who brought those beads?" Research Assistant/Consultant for **Beads of Life**, Dinka culture, interviewed on April 4, 2003 at the Canadian Museum of Civilization. The Maasai also asked this question during our fieldwork in 1984.

2. This could explain in part why certain peoples living near the coast, such as the Kamba and the Giriama, developed elaborate beading styles quite early.

3. Makueng Maliet, Research Assistant/Consultant for **Beads of Life**, Dinka culture.

4. Marie-Louise Labelle: "I encountered the same problem during my first stay in Maasai territory in 1982. The colours and sizes of the beads I brought, which were acquired from Parisian whole-salers, did not at all match those habitually used, and were refused. Only the white beads were successfully disposed of."

5. Labelle. Information gathered during fieldwork among the Maasai, 1984–1985.

6. Labelle, 1984–1985.

7. Sandra Klopper, "Women's Work, or Engendering the Art of Beadwork in Southern Africa," p. 30, quoted by Boram-Hays, p. 73.

8. Serge Tornay, ed., *Voir et Nommer les Couleurs* (Nanterre, France: Laboratoire d'Ethnologie et de Sociologie Comparative, 1978), Introduction.

9. "*Les diverses cultures humaines, en fonction de leur milieu naturel, de leur mode de vie, de leur histoire, accordent à la couleur une importance très variable. Peu d'entre elles, à l'instar de l'occidentale, considèrent la couleur comme une chose en soi, ou comme une perception coupée des autres impressions sensorielles.*" Ibid., p. XLIX.,

10. "*… la nature subjective de la perception … Nos sens nous fournissent une image du monde qui est conforme, non pas à la nature, mais à notre organisation biologique et à notre héritage culturel.*" Ibid., p. L.

11. Ibid., 1978.

12. Michel Pastoureau, *Blue: The History of a Color* (Princeton University Press, 2001), originally published as *Bleu : Histoire d'une couleur* (Paris: Seuil, 2000).

13. Tornay, 1978.

14. Jeremy Coote, "Marvels of Everyday Vision: The Anthropology of Aesthetics and the Cattle-Keeping Nilotes" in Jeremy Coote, Anthony Shelton, eds., *Anthropology, Art, and Aesthetics* (Oxford: Clarendon Press, 1992).

15. John Ryle, Sarah Errington (photographer), *Warriors of the White Nile: The Dinka*, photos by Sarah Errington, *Peoples of the Wild* (Amsterdam: Time-Life Books, 1982), quoted by Jeremy Coote, 1992.

16. According to Lienhardt, almost all of the colour vocabulary relates to livestock. "… the Dinka perceive colour, light and shade in the world around them in a manner which is intimately linked to the way in which they recognize the colour configurations in the coats of their livestock. If we omit their livestock-related vocabulary, we would be left with almost no means of describing visual experience in terms of colour, light and shade." Godfrey R. Lienhardt, *Divinity and Experience: The Religion of the Dinka* (Oxford: Clarendon Press, 1961), quoted by Serge Tornay, 1978.

17. Naming blue and green with a single term was common among the Nilotic societies of the southern Sudan and southern Ethiopia.

18. "For the color of the cows, it is *mangok*. You know in Dinka we don't have green cows or blue cows, we have blue like this, we have black and white, and grey … We don't have green also. It is not exactly green, it is greyish, and we call it also blue." Zeinab Mokwag and Makueng Maliet, Research Assistants/Consultants for **Beads of Life**, Dinka culture, interviewed on April 4, 2003 at the Canadian Museum of Civilization.

19. Marja-Liisa Swantz, *Blood, Milk, and Death: Body Symbols and the Power of Regeneration Among the Zaramo of Tanzania* (Westport: Bergin & Garvey, 1995), p. 70.

20. See Donna Klumpp's inventory of Maasai beadwork pattern names in relationship to configurations of the coats of cattle. Donna Klumpp: *Maasai Art and Society: Age and Sex, Time and Space, Cash and Cattle*, Ph.D. dissertation, Columbia University, New York, 1987.

21. Marguerite Poland, "Zulu Cattle: Colour Patterns and Imagery in the Names of Zulu Cattle," in *Zulu Treasures of Kings & Commoners: A Celebration of the Material Culture of the Zulu People* (The Local History Museums, 1996).

22. Ibid., p. 38.

23. Ibid., p. 40.

24. Dawn Costello, *Not Only for Its Beauty: Beadwork and Its Cultural Significance Among the Xhosa-Speaking Peoples* (Pretoria: University of South Africa, 1990).

25. Regina Twala, "Beads as Regulating the Social Life of the Zulu and Swazi," *African Studies*, Vol. 10:3, 1951.

26. Ibid., 1951.

27. Frank Jolles, "Traditional Zulu Beadwork of the Msinga Area," in *African Arts*, vol. 26(1) (Los Angeles: UCLA, 1993).

28. Twala, 1951.

29. C.M. Doke, et al., *English-Zulu/Zulu-English Dictionary* (Johannesburg: Witwatersrand University Press, 1990).

30. Twala, 1951.

31. Ibid., p. 117.

32. Ibid., p. 120.

33. Jolles, 1993.

34. Bongani N. Mthethwa, "Decoding Zulu Beadwork," in *Catching Winged Words: Oral Traditions and Education*, E.R. Sienaert and A.N. Bell, eds. (Durban: University of Natal Oral Documentation and Research Center, 1988), pp. 34–42.

35. Marilee Wood et al., *Zulu Treasures of Kings & Commoners: A Celebration of the Material Culture of the Zulu People* (The Local History Museums, 1996).

36. Research Assistant/Consultant for **Beads of Life** Zulu section.

37. The objective of the research was to obtain information on beadwork as well as reactions on some old Zulu beadwork pieces presented in the **Beads of Life** exhibition.

38. Sibongile Nene Research Assistant/Consultant for **Beads of Life** Zulu section, Interview of Bezemane Sibiya, Kwabiyela region, KwaZulu Natal, South Africa, August 2003.

39. Thus contradicting Marilee Wood, commenting on Frank Jolles' work: "Studying the early sources makes it clear that the various coloured beads do not act as an alphabet, but rather as ideograms: a particular bead, or combination of beads brings to mind something – often a natural object such as a bird – which sets off a series of associations which give meaning to the particular bead/s used (Jolles 1991:57-77)." Marilee Wood: 1996, ibid.

40. "*Les perles sont comme les lettres d'un alphabet, leurs rangs représentent des mots, leur nombre définit le genre et leur agencement annonce des phrases.*" Xavier Van der Stappen, *Les Maasaï, Pays – Histoire – Économie – Environnement – Croyances – Culture Matérielle* (La Renaissance du Livre, 2002), p. 152 & catalogue.

41. "*La ligne de perles oranges représente le père, chef de famille et propriétaire de l'objet, la ligne de perles bleues représente la tête de sa femme, les six rangs de perles jaunes symbolisent la prospérité de la famille. Les deux rangs rouges indiquent que la mère a un fils devenu Moran.*" Ibid., 2002.

42. "*… réfèrent à un conseil donné par les aînés : 'Ne vous attendez pas à ce que la vie soit uniforme, elle comporte des hauts et des bas.'* " Ibid., 2002.

AESTHETIC PRINCIPLES
OF BEADWORK

4

In a great many pieces of eastern and southern African beadwork, the choice of certain colours, colour combinations, designs and the use of space, reflects enduring aesthetic principles that are not affected by passing trends. Although each society has access to the same colours of beads and uses them to create similar designs, such as broken lines, stripes, circles, semi-circles, triangles, diamonds and checks, each creates its own style of beading. While the style is constantly affected by neighbouring influences, it is still easily recognizable and has become a "signature." It is likely that these different aesthetic principles not only correspond to the search for an ideal of harmony and order, but are also a profound reflection of the social and religious values integral to these societies.

Three colours are particularly important in most of the societies that practice beading in eastern and southern Africa. These are red, white and black (or dark blue in East Africa where the two colours often bear the same name). According to Pastoureau, these three colours are "the three basic colours of all ancient cultures."[1] They have long been available throughout Africa in a natural form in the environment, and still play a major role today in ceremonial and daily life.[2] As mineral powders, they have served to make body paints from the southern Sudan to South Africa. Among the Nuba of the Sudan, the Maasai and Samburu of Kenya, the Xhosa of South Africa and others, face paint was made from dye composed of chalk or ash mixed with water, charcoal, red clays of different colours, and fruit juices. Such face paints were used in numerous ceremonies including initiations, weddings, blessings and funeral rites, where they indicated the specific status of the participants.

Once glass beads were widely available, women naturally chose colours such as white, red and black or dark blue that had always been used to protect or indicate a particular status. Thus white beads would have replaced cowries and ostrich eggs. Black or dark blue beads would have taken the place of iron beads. In addition, bead choices tended to favour opposing colours so that strong colour contrasts could be created.

White is the main colour of a large number of ornaments. It was predominant in adornments of cowries and ostrich egg beads among the Turkana of northern Kenya and the San of Botswana. It also formed the "background" of the short skirts and belts worn by Zulu girls, and was equally predominant in the beadwork of the Xhosa and the Ndebele. The Kamba of Kenya also used it extensively in their adornments, and it was widely used in the skirts worn by the young Iraqw women of Tanzania.

Before the arrival of beads, white was used as body paint (Xhosa) or around the eyes (Maasai) during rites of passage, such as the initiation of youth. White makeup appears to have served as a protective element during the difficult and sometimes dangerous transitions of life. Among the Xhosa, the replacement of red ochre with white clay on the body indicated that something out of the ordinary had happened in the life of the wearer. According to Costello, youth undergoing initiation who painted their faces and bodies with white clay were excluded from the community because their association with it could delay their recovery.[3] On the faces of Maasai diviners, when they performed acts intended to protect people, it may have been used to invoke the world beyond.

In South Africa, particularly among the Zulu and the Xhosa, white was associated with the ancestors or "shades." The *sangomas* (diviners and healers) wore white beads in their hair and around their limbs, and put them on tools, such as fly whisks and medicine containers. The beads enabled them to communicate with the ancestors, who dictated diagnoses of patients' illnesses to them. Like white medicines, white beads are beneficial and pure and protect against evil. "White beads have an especially vital function in the traditionalist dress of *izangoma*, for they mediate the interactions between the bodies of *izangoma* and the *amadlozi* (ancestors) both to attract and control the forces of the spiritual realm."[4]

The association of white with benevolence is nearly universal throughout eastern and southern Africa. In the southern region, its particular association with the world of the ancestors

Figure 40 Dumile Mtshali, a Zulu *sangoma* (diviner/healer), wears white beads in her hair to help her communicate with her ancestors. South Africa, 2003.

Photo: Sibongile Nene, Research Assistant/Consultant for **Beads of Life**, Zulu section has probably played a role in the predominance of white in many of the adornments worn by the region's peoples.

In virtually all areas of eastern and southern Africa, red was worn as a form of body paint designed to enhance beauty both on a daily basis and during ceremonies. Red paint was obtained by mixing various mineral powders with animal fat or water. The paint was sometimes applied in designs that enhanced facial features, as among the Samburu. In Maasai ceremonies, red ochre helped to distinguish the main participants of the ritual: their ornaments, foreheads and heads were smeared with *olkaria*, a red ochre powder obtained in local shops and once traded with neighbouring peoples.

The Maasai and the Samburu often associated red with blood. This is not surprising considering the important ritual role of the blood of livestock, both in ceremonies, where it was shared by the participants, and in situations of temporary vulnerability (initiation, motherhood, famine, etc.) that required its consumption. It was a source of life and strength, and as such, was generally reserved for the youth, who represent the future of the group.

The Xhosa also painted their bodies and clothing with red ochre, a colour which Dawn Costello calls the "symbol of normality," or the "blood of the earth," favoured by the ancestors. During rites aimed at introducing a newborn to its ancestors, the child and its mother were smeared with red ochre. In earlier times, when a young Xhosa woman knew she was going to be married, she was required to paint her entire body, save the face, with red ochre. On the other hand, ochre was avoided during periods of mourning, and was reintroduced only after the end of this period, following a ritual or a sacrifice to the ancestors.[5]

According to Berglund as well, among the Zulu red was associated with the ancestors. It was also associated with blood, menstruation and motherhood,[6] which Carol Boram-Hays qualifies as "times of transformation and transition, when human life can be brought from the spiritual realm of the *amadlozi* (ancestors) into the physical realm … Seen as a symbol of transition and transformation, the function of red in the costume and regalia of *izangoma* becomes apparent. *Izangoma*, as possessed by ancestors of the spiritual world, are in a transient state between the physical and spiritual realms. The red beads in the dress of an *isangoma* are, thereby, intended to promote the transitional state of the body used by the *amadlozi* to cross between the physical and spiritual realms."[7]

Black (or sometimes dark blue in East Africa) had different connotations, depending on the region. Although this colour played a clearly beneficial role in eastern Africa, its significance and uses were more complex in the larger region of southern Africa. Victor Turner has suggested that "black tends to become an auspicious color in regions where water is short, for the black clouds bring fertility and growth. In regions where water is plentiful and food more or less abundant, black may well be inauspicious."[8]

Animals that are black in colour were often chosen for certain sacrifices aimed at bringing rain in the southern Sudan. In East Africa, black (or dark blue) was also the colour most often associated with God, who lives in the sky and brings rain, the source of life. Among the Oromo, the term "black," *gurraaca*, also describes the colour of water. The Oromo deity *Waaqa* is considered to be black in colour ("*God is black. Black is the sign of holiness and of purity.*"[9]), but the term "black" could also evoke infinity and mystery.[10] Similarly, the Maasai God is called *Enkai narok*, the "Black God," who is good and sends rain. In addition, one of the Booran clans is known as the "People of the Black Bead."[11]

Figure 41 Maasai bride smeared with red ochre. Kenya, 1985.

Photo: Marie-Louise Labelle

The use of dark blue beads extends to the seeking of divine protection, and both the Oromo and the Maasai wore necklaces of dark blue beads (*emurt narok*) around their necks when they prayed to God. At the centre of their ceremonial village (*emanyata*), young Maasai initiates raised a pole of sacred olive wood topped with a flag of blue fabric; dark blue beads were coiled around the end of the pole. In addition, dark blue beads were hung at the entrance to each house in the ceremonial village to protect its inhabitants. In East Africa, blue beads were widely used by recent initiates, either around their necks or their foreheads, and in some places, blue beads adorned gourds containing milk, the vital liquid.

In many parts of East Africa, the colour black (or dark blue) also indicated seniority or high status. Among the Maasai, wooden staffs and capes of black animal skin (the latter replaced today with blue fabric) designated spokespersons for different age sets, as well as diviners and prophets. Turkana women smeared themselves with wood charcoal to identify themselves as mature women. Women also decorated their aprons with black iron beads to indicate their status as mothers, whereas young girls wore aprons adorned with ostrich egg beads. Among the Kamba as well, the use of blue beads was the prerogative of married and mature women, while red and white beads were reserved for young girls.[12]

In southern Africa, black has different meanings. It is often considered a harmful colour, and many researchers have suggested that its presence in beaded adornments indicates a "negative message." This corroborates the analysis made by Ingo Lambrecht in the text accompanying the 2002 exhibition **Art and Oracle: African Art and Rituals of Divination** at the

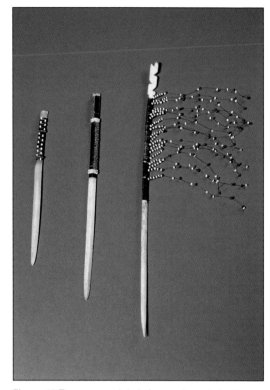

Figure 42 These woman's hairpins are decorated with beads in the colours red, white and blue.

Photo: © Canadian Museum of Civilization, Steven Darby

From left to right:

Hairpin
Zulu, South Africa
Late 19th or early 20th century
Bone, glass beads and animal hair
15.8 cm (l) x 0.3 cm (w)
Redpath Museum, Montreal 04981.01

Hairpin
Zulu, South Africa
Late 19th or early 20th century
Bone, glass beads and animal hair
21 cm (l) x 0.4 cm (w)
Vancouver Museum F663 FE422

Hairpin
Zulu, South Africa
Late 19th or early 20th century
Bone, glass beads and animal hair
28 cm (l) x 10 cm (w)
Provincial Museum of Alberta, Edmonton H62.2.327

Metropolitan Museum of Art. According to Lambrecht, "black medicine (used by *Sangomas*) is used to represent darkness, night, danger, and difficulties."[13] Much earlier, Krige noted that black medicines provided renewed strength to the unwell, but had to be followed by white medicines to wash away their ill effects.[14] Used in clothing and adornments, black does not seem to express such meanings. Consider, for example, the traditional black skin skirts worn by married Zulu women, the black shields that once distinguished young Zulu warriors, and the large number of beaded ornaments in southern Africa that for a century have included black, acknowledging its important aesthetic role in creating designs and contrasts, while also ensuring the general harmony of the composition. It is difficult to believe that these ornaments would have included a colour with strong negative connotations. Certain sources also mention[15] that among the Nguni peoples, as in East Africa, black could evoke a sky heavy with rain, thus abundance and fertility. It could also be tied to the world of the ancestors, with the assumption that this colour could help to ensure protection.[16]

The three colours, red, white and black (blue), do not work alone, but through combinations of two or three.[17] The repeated use of the combination of black (or blue), red and

Figure 43

Necklace
Afar, Ethiopia
Second half of the 20th century
Glass beads, aluminum, cowries, plant fibre and plastic button
31 cm (l) x 19 cm (w)

Anthropology Department, Université de Montréal 61.296
Photo: © Canadian Museum of Civilization, Steven Darby

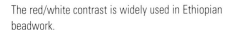
The red/white contrast is widely used in Ethiopian beadwork.

Figure 44

Filekebela
Pendant
Afar, Ethiopia
Second half of the 20th century
Glass beads, animal hide, cowries and plant fibre
22 cm (l) x 7.5 cm (w)

Anthropology Department, Université de Montréal 61.293
Photo: © Canadian Museum of Civilization, Steven Darby

white in beadwork is notable, particularly in the earliest beaded ornaments from southern Africa during the nineteenth century (Figure 42), and East African beadwork during a large part of the twentieth century. We will now examine some examples of these colour combinations and their possible correspondence with cultural traits of the societies in which they were used.

In Ethiopia, particularly in the South, the use of two contrasting colours in beadwork was common. This is seen on the red and white ornaments worn by Afar girls, and the beadwork of the Arsi Oromo, where the colour scheme often opposes red and white or white and blue (Figures 43 to 46). Red and yellow beads (yellow glass beads probably replacing amber ones) were the dominant colours in the necklaces of Booran and Gabra women and, according to Aneesa Kassam, signified fertility and good health. Also according to Kassam, among the Oromo the three colours black/blue, red and white represented the vital fluids, i.e. water, blood and milk respectively.[18] But the possible justifications for these contrasts perhaps go even further.

In *Symbolic Structures in Turkana Religion*, Van der Jagt discusses the systems of contrasting elements that governed the society of Turkana herdsmen. These systems of opposites are

Figure 45

Hair Ornament
Arsi Oromo, Ethiopia
Second half of the 20th century
Glass beads, cowries, animal hide, plant fibre and plastic button
41 cm (l) x 9.5 cm (w)
Photo: © Canadian Museum of Civilization, CMC-2002.20.4, Steven Darby, T2004-280

Figure 46

Necklace
Arsi Oromo, Ethiopia
Second half of the 20th century
Glass beads, plastic buttons, animal hide, metal, cowries and plant fibre
41 cm (l) x 32 cm (w)
Anthropology Department, Université de Montréal 61.257
Photo: © Canadian Museum of Civilization, Steven Darby

The red/white contrast is widely used in Ethiopian beadwork.

common to many pastoral societies in East Africa. Such "binary structures" concern the alternation of male generations, (the "Stones" and the "Leopards"), the opposed age sets of the "Left Hand" and the "Right Hand," the opposing compass points in which West is malevolent and East is benevolent, the distinction between the main village in which the first wife of the family head resides and the secondary village of the second wife, the opposition between the semi-circular day hut and the round night hut, the opposition of the masculine and feminine worlds, and above all, the existence of the two opposing spiritual principles, *Akuj* and *Ekipe*. *Akuj* is a supernatural force that distributes rain and lives in the sky. It is a source of life, characterized by a strong luminosity and the colour white. *Ekipe*, by contrast, causes death and destruction, lives in dark, subterranean, arid places, and is represented by black and red. Turkana beadwork is characterized by the opposition of strong contrasts of white with black (or dark blue) and of white with red. The most common designs, whether they are found on the ornaments and skirts of young girls and women, or on more everyday objects like milk containers (Figure 48), are the circle, the semi-circle (or arch), and sometimes the rectangle. These motifs, called *eboli* in the singular and *ngibolyo* in the plural (this term designating all motifs of beads sewn to a stiff skin, not a particular pattern), always used in a series. They are aligned on the surface of the leather in the manner of circular and semi-circular houses spread throughout the arid landscape of northern Kenya, but not necessarily representing them.

Figure 47 Simple contrasts between blue and white, and yellow and red, predominate in the adornments of Arbore women. Ethiopia, 2000.

Photo: Ivo Romein (www.go.to/ethiopianet)

Figure 48 This container has been decorated with the *eboli* beaded pattern in the shape of an arch.

Akurum
Container
Turkana, Kenya
Second half of the 20th century
Wood, goatskin or sheepskin, glass beads, plant fibre, cowries and pigments
64 cm (h), 21 cm (d)

University of Alberta Art and Artifact Collection Museums and Collections Services, Edmonton
983.57.1.30 a,b
Photo: © Canadian Museum of Civilization, Steven Darby

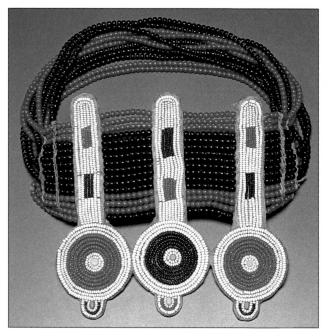

Figure 49 Contrasts of colours in Turkana beadwork could refer to socio-religious principles.

Ngakoromwa Ngibolio
Necklace
Turkana, Kenya
Second half of the 20th century
Glass beads, goat or sheep hide and plant fibre
20.3 cm (l), 28.6 cm (d)

Textile Museum of Canada, Toronto
T94.2188a
Photo: © Canadian Museum of Civilization, Steven Darby

The *abuo*[19] skirt in figure 129 shows an excellent example of the way these contrasts are expressed, with opposing circles of blue and white, and red and white. Similar contrasts can also be seen in the necklaces of young girls of marriageable age, *ngakoromwa ngibolio* (Figure 49). Today, with the adoption of green, yellow, orange, etc., this system of simple contrasts has been altered.

The triad of red, white and black (or blue) has also been central in the beadwork of the Maasai and the Samburu for more than a century. In this case also, these colour contrasts, when in the form of natural materials, played a major role in numerous rituals and ceremonies, and were imbued with meaning for the participants. Red, associated with blood, was reserved for youth, and implied potential life; white sometimes marked a state of transition between two states (initiation for example); and black (or dark blue) implied seniority, maturity or anything related to the divine.

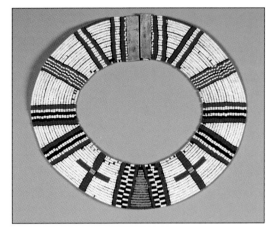

Figure 50 White formed the background of most Kamba ornaments, with coloured accents in red and blue, and later yellow, orange and green.

Necklace
Kamba, Kenya
Second half of the 20th century
Glass beads, iron and aluminum
24.4 cm (l) x 21.6 cm (w)
Glenbow Museum, Calgary FF 86
Photo: © Canadian Museum of Civilization, Steven Darby

These contrasts also had a religious significance. The red God is opposed to the black God, just as in the social structure, the two original clan divisions are named "Red Ox" and "Black Cow." It is thus not surprising to find these contrasts in the beadwork. Yet, what characterizes the associations of colours in Maasai beadwork in the second half of the twentieth century is the combination of the colours blue/orange and green/red, separated by white. Since orange and green beads were adopted much later by Maasai women, it is conceivable that they were used as equivalents of red and blue respectively, and that in this series of five colours, it is in fact the contrast blue/red, separated by white, that is always repeated.[20] (Figure 51)

It is tempting to suggest that this triad of colours in beadwork is related to some Maasai social structures such as the combination of opposites, and the road from immaturity (red) towards seniority (blue/black), with white as a transition. The Maasai, however, insist that the coloured motifs of their beadwork have no significance, and they are obviously right. It is, in fact, only the three colours themselves that have ritual functions, when they are used alone or in twos to manifest specific states of being, or when they play a protective or status-indicating role as in the case of blue beads used for prayer or to protect young initiates. Among the Samburu, these blue beads are sometimes replaced by green ones since they use green as an equivalent of blue in a ceremonial context. Samburu women make a clear distinction between "beads for decoration" (beads of all colours used on a daily basis in their adornments) and "beads of tradition" (meaning those imbued with a traditional function). To ascribe an immutable meaning to the combination of the five colours used by the Maasai thus becomes an error of perception, since it is necessary to take into account not only the constant adoption of new colours, but also the purely practical aspect of the use of one colour for ritual purposes, which has to be visible and clear to all. If this colour is mixed with other colours, it loses its function and meaning. And, if it is possible that these aesthetic rules of beadwork are based on socio-religious concepts, it is in a form that is constantly renewed and modified, making their detection particularly difficult today. It is notable that the aesthetic of the Maasai rests upon its complementary nature,[21] which makes it compulsory that each unit of a pair of earrings, for example, be different from the other (Figure 52).

Figure 51 The white/red/blue triad has been enhanced with orange and green.

Imankeek
Necklaces
Maasai, Kenya
Second half of the 20th century
Glass beads, animal hide, iron and plastic
35.8 cm (overall circumference)
Photo: © Canadian Museum of Civilization, CMC-1974-105-004, Steven Darby, T2004-281

The combination of black (blue)/white/red is not limited to the Maasai, but was common among many other peoples of East Africa, each of which favoured one contrast more than another, depending on its priorities.

In Tanzania as well, these three colours played an important role, notably in initiation rites. In her study of Zaramo initiation, M. L. Swantz notes the importance of what she calls "organic" colours, those associated with substances basic to the human body and linked to the primary functions of life. Black represented hair and body hair, red represented menstrual blood and white represented semen. At all stages in the initiation of boys and girls, these colours were used in the form of trees and plants such as tri-coloured corn, fruits, etc. as well as earth, soot, and beads. A Zaramo girl undergoing initiation placed one bead of each of the three colours under her tongue, and her body was smeared with each of them as well, in the form of coloured powders. During ceremonies related to the end of her period of seclusion, the young girl wore a necklace in which these three colours were repeated.[22] (Figure 53)

One of the best-known beaded garments in Tanzania, especially since its appearance in the catalogue, *Africa, the Art of a Continent*,[23] is the skirt made by young Iraqw girls during the period of seclusion that was part of the *marmo* initiation rite (Figure 69). This skirt also bore the three colours, white, red and blue. The cosmology of the Iraqw people refers to two opposing spirits, the benevolent *Lo'a*, associated with the sky, the sun and rain, is warm, brilliant, therefore white; and *Netlangw*, harmful "spirits of below" associated with the earth (red), and with streambeds, springs and dampness, who are dark (and thus black or dark blue) and cold.[24]

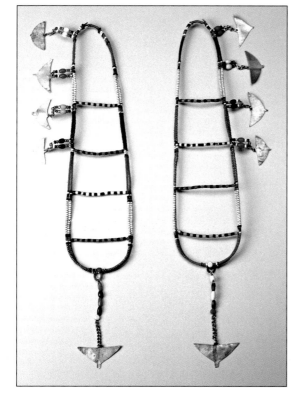

Figure 52 The colours in each earring complement one another.

Imuna
Earrings
Maasai, Kenya
Second half of the 20th century
Glass beads, iron and aluminum
Each: 34.5 cm (l) x 7 cm (w)
University of Alberta Art and Artifact Collection
Museums and Collections Services, Edmonton
983.57.1.12-ab
Photo: © Canadian Museum of Civilization, Steven Darby

The widespread use of white on these skirts seems to correspond to a desire for protection by invoking the spirit *Lo'a*, while also reflecting the purity of young girls. Among the Iraqw, the colour white also plays an important role in certain purification rituals, or healing rituals aimed at "whitening disease."[25] The contrasts of white/red and white/dark blue are thus perhaps references to Iraqw cosmology: *Lo'a*, the benevolent spirit, is opposed to *Netlangw*, the red or dark blue harmful spirits. These colours would thus be chosen, not only for their protective role, but also for the way in which they reflected recognition of the benevolent and harmful spirits that affect all stages of life.

Farther to the south, these characteristics also exist, although sometimes in different forms. For example, the Tonga women of the Zambezi Valley combined these three colours together perfectly in their unique beadwork (Figure 54). Originally related to Zulu people, the Tonga practiced a rain cult, which may explain their use of dark blue (their God is sometimes associated with rain). They also honoured the "shades" (or ancestors' spirits), which could be evoked by the colour white, also widely used in initiation ceremonies. Finally, they smeared the bodies of their young women with red ochre.

Photographs that would enable us to determine the primary bead-colour choices of the Zulu do not exist. We must rely on descriptions and sketches left by early European explorers. These descriptions are sometimes fragmentary and do not always give us an idea of the entire costume. Nonetheless, illustrations by Angas suggest the predominance of ornaments bearing strong contrasts of red and white. Similarly, as seen in many of the pieces in Canadian museums,

Figure 53 Young Zaramo girls wore a necklace of this type when their initiation (*mwali*) was completed. The three protective colours refer to blood, semen and hair.

Necklace
Zaramo?, Tanzania
First half of the 20th century
Glass beads and plant fibre
50 cm (l) x 7.5 cm (w)
Redpath Museum, Montreal 03861
Photo: © Canadian Museum of Civilization, Steven Darby

a large portion of the beaded Zulu ornaments collected at the end of the nineteenth century display a marked use of contrasts of blue, red and white (Figures 55 and 56). Colours diversified very quickly, blurring these trends. Green, pink (as already noted, pink is called "poor red" in the Zulu language), yellow, etc., which made their appearance simultaneously with, or after, beads of blue, red and white, were also used to create strong contrasts, perhaps due to their equivalency to blue, white and red (Figure 57). The triad of black/white/red has a particular significance in the practice of divination. According to Lambrecht, red "is the bridging color of transformation" between black medicine that represents, as we have already seen, danger and storms, and white that "refers to health, purity, and success." Also according to Lambrecht, "The method of cure begins with detoxification (through the power of the black medicine), followed by a transformation (using the red medicine), and ending with a strengthening of the client (with the white medicine)."[26] The use of these three colours is found in the costumes of Zulu women. In earlier times, only young pre-pubescent girls wore short white aprons. Following puberty, they donned short red aprons, and at marriage, the black *isidwaba* skirt. This colour hierarchy in female skirts can still be seen in the ceremonial dress of the Shembe church (see Chapter 6). The order of the colour triad is different in East Africa where, as we have seen, white appears as a colour of transition, between red, which is synonymous with immaturity, and blue, which is the colour of seniority and the divine.

The beadwork produced by Xhosa-speaking peoples (Bomvana, Mfengu, Xhosa proper, etc.) in the late nineteenth century plays resolutely upon the contrasts between white and black, white and red, and all three colours combined. The black/white contrast is found in important Xhosa protective ornaments such as the *izitsaba* anklets (Figure 58), the *incebeta* chest covering worn by married women, and the short *inkciyo* skirts of young girls. Mfengu beadwork, which for historical reasons is found in abundance in many collections, uses the

Figure 54 Tonga beadwork often featured the triad of blue, red and white.

Ndeke
Apron
Tonga, Zimbabwe
Second half of the 20th century
Cloth, plant fibre and glass beads
23 cm (w) x 18 cm (l); with straps: 38 cm (l)

On loan from the William and Barbara McCann Collection
Photo: © Canadian Museum of Civilization, Steven Darby

Figure 55

Ulimi
Necklace
Zulu, South Africa
Late 19th or early 20th century
Glass beads and plant fibre
15 cm (l) x 17.5 cm (w), 44.7 cm (circumference)
New Brunswick Museum, Saint John 5367
Photo: © Canadian Museum of Civilization,
Steven Darby

Figure 56

Ishungu
Container
Zulu, South Africa
Late 19th or early 20th century
Gourd, glass beads and plant fibre
10 cm (h), 7 cm (d)
Manitoba Museum, Winnipeg H6.24.53
Photo: © Canadian Museum of Civilization,
Steven Darby

Many pieces of Zulu beadwork from the end
of the 19th century are characterized by the
combination of blue (or black), white and red.

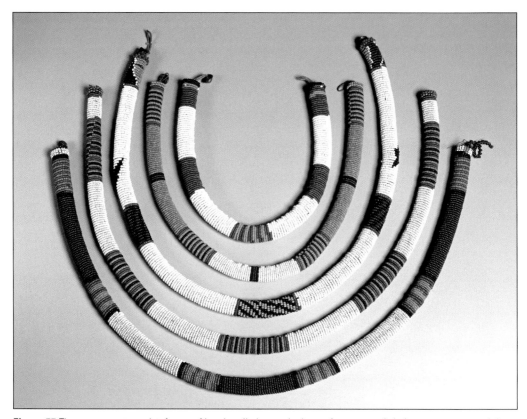

Figure 57 These ornaments made of rows of beads coiled around a base of compressed cloth were worn around the head, neck and waist of young people.

Photo: © Canadian Museum of Civilization, Steven Darby

From top to bottom:

Umgingqo
Necklace
Zulu, South Africa
Late 19th or early 20th century
Glass beads, plant fibre and brass button
45 cm (l) x 2.3 cm (w)
Redpath Museum, Montreal 0399.02

Umgingqo
Necklace
Zulu, South Africa
Late 19th or early 20th century
Glass beads, plant fibre and brass buttons
76 cm (l), 2 cm (d)
Redpath Museum, Montréal 0399.01

Umgingqo
Necklace
Zulu, South Africa
Late 19th or early 20th century
Glass beads, plant fibre and brass button
79.7 cm (l), 2.2 cm (d)
Provincial Museum of Alberta, Edmonton — H79.31.9

Umgingqo
Necklace
Zulu, South Africa
Late 19th or early 20th century
Glass beads and plant fibre
68 cm (l) x 2.8 cm (w)
Glenbow Museum, Calgary FX23b

Umgingqo
Necklace
Zulu, South Africa
Late 19th or early 20th century
Glass beads and plant fibre
76 cm (l), 1.8 cm (d)
Vancouver Museum FE322 (F532)

"triad" by emphasizing blue, often as a background colour, upon which designs of red and white lozenges stand out (Figure 59). In other cases, and often on the short skirts of young girls, white forms the background while designs of red and black (or blue) stand out against it. Most of the designs are lozenges, broken lines, triangles, and stripes (Figure 60). The beadwork of the Hlubi, who are Xhosa-speaking but neighbours of the Zulu and thus influenced by their style, is characterized by the alternating of black with a bright colour, on a white background (Figures 61 and 62).

During the twentieth century, Xhosa-speaking women incorporated other colours such as orange, green and yellow. The original designs remained however, although they were also refined, sometimes achieving a sort of mannerism when compared with the "cruder" designs that characterized earlier beadwork (Figure 63). Also visually important are the mother-of-pearl buttons prevalent in Xhosa beadwork and employed either as an accent in the articulations of the designs and parts of the ornament, or used lavishly on shawls or felt turbans, producing a

Figure 58 The contrast of white and black predominates on Xhosa ornaments of the late 19th century, particularly on adornments that indicate status.

Izitsaba
Anklets
Xhosa, South Africa
First half of the 20th century
Glass beads, sinew and animal hide
21.6 cm (l) x 7.7 cm (w); 21 cm (l) x 7.9 cm (w)
Photo: © Canadian Museum of Civilization, CMC-B-III-55-a/b, Steven Darby, T2004-282

particularly striking decorative effect (Figure 64). It is possible that these buttons are the modern equivalent of cowries or ostrich eggshell beads, which would once have played a protective role.

Such contrasts are therefore one of the essential components of eastern and southern African beadwork. Not only do they correspond to values that are profoundly anchored in the society itself, but they also helped beadworkers to create an optimal visual effect.

With the greater availability of glass beads, women began to "fill" the leather or fibre surface of garments and ornaments to an even greater extent. On some larger pieces of clothing

Figure 59

Iphoco
Apron and Belt
Mfengu, South Africa
Late 19th or early 20th century
Glass beads, sinew and mother-of-pearl buttons
Belt portion: 58.6 cm (l) x 7.6 cm (w)
Apron portion: 17.8 cm (l) x 36 cm (w)
Photo: © Canadian Museum of Civilization, CMC-1970.035.030 & 1970.035.023, Steven Darby, T2004-283

such as capes or skirts, creativity was given free rein, resulting in veritable works of art in which the search for balance and harmony of the forms and colours was predominant. Beads finally enabled the creation of elaborate designs, and some more recent examples include figurative elements (Figure 65). Each society expresses its signature in its particular choice of designs, as well as in the way in which the space of the underlying surface is supported and organized.

These characteristics differentiate the beadwork of eastern Africa from that of southern Africa and, to an even greater extent, the beadwork of pastoral peoples from that of agriculturalists. Among nomadic or semi-nomadic pastoralists, we find the predominance of the line, creating empty "open" spaces, or sometimes, as among the Turkana or the San, clusters of beads that are isolated from one another on the leather background. By contrast, surfaces saturated with designs defining "closed" spaces predominate among settled agriculturalists. Is this the result of less widespread access to beads among pastoral peoples, and thus of their more limited use? Or is it the expression of a certain ideal, tied to a particular way of looking at the management of their lands? Among pastoralists, space is unlimited, and no one may claim the land; instead, it is used equally by one and all. The same concept applies to hunter-gatherers. Among sedentary farmers however, the idea of defining territory is prevalent.

Can we also consider beaded space as a representation of the space of life, either real, in the manner of a geographical map, or imaginary, as in "laying out" the greater principles of a

Figure 60

Ingxowa
Bags
Mfengu, South Africa
Late 19th or early 20th century
Cloth, animal hide, sinew and glass
beads
Bag on left: 21cm (l) x 13.5 cm (w)
Bag on right: 42.8 cm (l) x 15.7 cm (w)

Museum of Anthropology, University of
British Columbia, Vancouver K5.91 (left)
Photo: © Canadian Museum of Civilization,
CMC-1970.035.016 (right), Steven Darby,
T2004-284

society? We will look at several examples of the way space is treated in women's garments from eastern and southern Africa.

The first example is the goatskin or sheepskin skirt (*olekesana*) of Maasai women (Figure 66). This skirt was part of required dress for married women, and was worn from the day of their marriage to the day of their death. This skirt had great importance within the ceremonial cycle, and until very recently was worn by the women during important ceremonies where it served as an active element in certain rituals aimed at protecting people.

These skirts bear very specific designs. In most cases, the patterns, placed in the center of the skirt, consist of vertical lines or "chevrons" arranged in parallel rows. Each of these lines is created in keeping with the code of "classic" Maasai colour schemes such as green/red/white/blue/orange. Beads of another sort, the flat *entepei* beads and the ovoid *entutai* beads, are also used to create lines emphasizing the pattern even further. The decorations also follow the

Figure 61

Apron?
Hlubi, South Africa
Late 19th or early 20th century
Glass beads, plant fibre and brass buttons
96.3 cm (circumference), 5.5 cm (w), 32 cm (d)
Vancouver Museum FE603
Photo: © Canadian Museum of Civilization, Steven Darby

Figure 62

Necklace
Hlubi, South Africa
Late 19th or early 20th century
Glass beads, plant fibre, brass buttons, metal and mirror
46.3 cm (l), 60 cm (circumference)
Kelowna Museum E.995.040.008
Photo: © Canadian Museum of Civilization, Steven Darby

sides and lower border of the skirt, especially the cut-outs indicating the status of married woman (see Chapter 5). When describing their beadwork, Maasai women mention "divisions," "borders," "broken" lines, and thus lines in general and not closed forms such as triangles and circles.[27]

The broken line outlining triangles and lines in half-moon form are also seen on the traditional *olbene* leather bag that women used in earlier times to hold their personal possessions (Figure 67). These designs are similar to the brand marks on animals that are intended to distinguish the livestock of different clans. These pure lines, which help to create a more willowy silhouette, an aesthetic ideal among the Maasai, can also be seen during the dances of young people, during which they effect vertical jumps or dance and march in perfect lines. Most Maasai beadwork is based upon an accumulation of parallel lines that occasionally define the designs of such items as necklaces (concentric lines), bracelets, the elongated earrings featuring "projections" that rise up and the headbands of young girls with very high rods evoking an aeroplane or an antenna. The entire costume of the Maasai, and that of the Nilotic peoples in general, reflects an aerial character that may recall the origins claimed by these peoples, i.e. the sky and God who lives there (Figure 68). We

Figure 63

Amapasi
Necklace
Xhosa, South Africa
Second half of the 20th century
Glass beads, sinew and mother-of-pearl buttons
64.5 cm (l) x 20.8 cm (w)
Photo: © Canadian Museum of Civilization, CMC-B-III-44, Steven Darby, T2004-285

have only to consider the famous male corsets of the Dinka with their vertical projection imitating a cow horn flinging itself skyward (thus its name *tung*: "horn"). The rejection of closed spaces could express the pastoral ideal, and thus a rejection of sedentary life and the chopping up of land into private plots. Since community development of their lands by the Maasai is nearly a thing of the past, the tendency to avoid closed spaces in beadwork is, in fact, currently changing. As a result, designs have become more defined, while at the same time, colours are multiplying. This represents a distancing from the traditional aesthetic scheme that was used by the Maasai for more than a century.

A different spirit prevailed on the skirts made by young Iraqw girls of northern Tanzania during their period of seclusion (Figure 69). The Iraqw are a people of the Cushitic language group who practice agriculture on plateaus. Their fields rise in terraces along ridges that are separated by deep valleys in which rivers flow. Robert Thornton has devoted a book to a description of the ritualization of space among the Iraqw, from the interior of the home and its surroundings, to the fields and lands stretching away into the distance.[28] Each of these spaces, whether private or communal, corresponds to formal attitudes that were scrupulously observed by the inhabitants. Specific rituals were held at each of the "frontiers" between these spaces, and individuals were made responsible for guarding these borders. The slopes of the ridges facing north were associated with evil and witchcraft, and metaphorically represented the abode of evil people, as opposed to the slopes exposed to the sun, which were associated with "good people." The ritualization of space among the Iraqw could thus have an impact on the way in which space was organized and outlined on the above-noted skirts.

Young Iraqw girls beginning their seclusion would bring with them a leather cape devoid of decoration. During their seclusion, they were required to embroider it with beads (natural materials would have been used before glass beads were available). When they emerged from seclusion, they wore these skirts during the dances celebrating their new status as women of marriageable age. Following marriage, women became active members of the community.[29] These skirts use the three colours of the blue/red/white triad and are richly decorated, leaving very little empty space. What makes these skirts so interesting and unique is that their style of beadwork, although close to that of the neighbouring Maasai and Datoga, integrates other styles, such as the ones used by people farther south. In addition, while not strictly figurative, they use very specific motifs that are not found on other beaded ornaments within the region or elsewhere.

An examination of several specimens of these skirts enables us to distinguish their commonalities in the use of colour, motifs and spatial organization. The example in the collection of the Royal Ontario Museum conforms to the principles of the treatment of space seen in other skirts.[30]

The surface of these skirts is divided vertically into three sections, the central section being heavily decorated with white beads, thus rendering it much brighter than the other two parts.

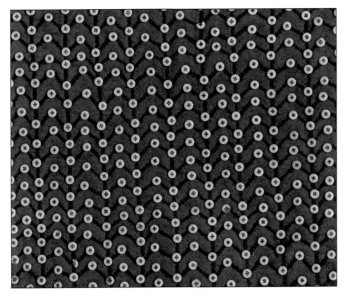

Figure 64

Ibhayi (detail)
Shawl with Button Trim
Mfengu?, South Africa
Late 19th or early 20th century
Cloth, glass or china buttons, fibre,
glass beads and metal
132.5 cm (l) x 124.0 cm (w)
Royal Ontario Museum 972.191.24.1
With the permission of the Royal Ontario
Museum © ROM

The sections on each side are meant to appear in front of the body, one section overlapping the other.[31] The central section appears at the back of the woman's body. The placement of the most heavily decorated part at the back is a common feature on many East African women's skirts and capes. These three vertical sections, with the much brighter central section often bearing figures of suns, seem to follow what was noticed by Thornton: that the slopes exposed to the south, i.e. to the sun, were opposed to the dark ones exposed to the north.

In addition to these vertical divisions, there are also three main horizontal sections, each decorated differently. Alternating stripes of white and red, white and blue, or even blue and red, dominate the top and bottom sections of the skirt in different fashions. As the earlier analysis of colours suggests, these could evoke the two opposing spirits, *Lo'a* and *Netlaang*, and, through them, the spiritual universe. However, the centre bottom section is white only.

Underneath the top zone are spaces decorated with motifs. Since these spaces appear in strategic locations of the body, they no doubt play an important role in the representation of

Figure 65 Xhosa beadwork sometimes includes stylized human figures, as can be seen in this figure of a woman in her traditional skirt.

Iphoco (detail)
Necklace
Xhosa, South Africa
Second half of the 20th century
Glass beads, sinew and mother-of-pearl buttons
25.7 cm (l) x 25.5 cm (w), 15.2 cm (d)
Photo: © Canadian Museum of Civilization, CMC-B-III-17, Steven Darby, T2004-286

Figure 66 Designs on Maasai skirts may have been inspired by traditional patterns used in marking livestock.

Olokesana
Skirt
Maasai, Kenya
Second half of the 20th century
Goat skin, glass beads, buttons, ochre and plant fibre
130 cm (w) x 97 cm (l)

University of Alberta Art and Artifact Collection
Museums and Collections Services, Edmonton 983.57.1.16
Photo: © Canadian Museum of Civilization, Steven Darby

a young girl's fertility and her future role as mother, householder and active member of the community. They are also the most visible parts of the skirt. The motifs are of two types: circles and lines. The circles often have rays, thus evoking suns, and they are sometimes divided into three or six parts. On this particular skirt, since the divided circles include rays, they are also suns. These motifs could refer to different religious or domestic elements of the Iraqw universe. The sun is one of the representations of the spirit *Lo'a*. The partitioned circle could be a representation of the traditional round house (*do*), which was divided into several spaces, each with a precise function. Most of the skirts also have zigzags or wavy lines that could depict roads or rivers, perhaps symbolizing, in turn, the subterranean *Netlaang* spirits (which are often depicted by streams). The lines in the form of crenellations define open or closed spaces. They could depict community spaces, for example the courtyards around the houses, or more likely, fields.

In conclusion, this skirt could represent the living space of the future married woman, her house, neighbourhood and fields, while also being closely intertwined with the supernatural world of the opposing spirits *Lo'a* and *Netlangw*. It can be read like a map, an aerial view of the physical and spiritual space of the Iraqw. The young girl arrives with an empty map (an

Figure 67

Olbene
Bag
Maasai, Kenya
Second half of the 20th century
Cow hide, glass beads, iron and plant fibre
53 cm (l) x 43 cm (w)

University of Alberta Art and Artifact Collection
Museums and Collections Services, Edmonton 983.57.1.13
Photo: © Canadian Museum of Civilization, Steven Darby

undecorated skin) and leaves with a detailed plan of her future life. At a time when the *marmo* ritual is probably no longer practiced, having been abolished during the 1930s, and when Iraqw women only make extremely simplified versions of these skirts to sell to tourists,[32] this analysis only suggests interpretations of the forms, colours and the unique treatment of space in beadwork created by Iraqw women.

Representation is more certain in other beaded ornaments, especially those of the Kamba, an agricultural Bantu people of Kenya who maintained close contacts in the past with Arab merchants from the coast. Kamba beadwork displays motifs such as arrowheads, rectangles, triangles, diamonds and crosses made to stand out against a white background (Figure 70). These motifs are shared with certain types of beadwork seen among peoples living closer to the shores of the Indian Ocean, the Giriama for example. The creation of these designs is not new to the Kamba since the ceremonial wooden staffs once used in boys' initiation rites were engraved by the elders with designs and signs that the boys and girls had to decipher in a game similar to charades. Circles represented the sun, spots represented the stars, and there were moons, arrows, and animals such as the snake, lizard and tortoise. The girls later carried pieces of these staffs around their necks, along with an iron bead taken from the skirt of a married woman.[33] Indeed, many pieces of Kamba beadwork, with their perfect alignment of figures,

Figure 68 Maasai girl with her earrings raised for dancing. Maasailand, Kenya, 1985.

Photo: Marie-Louise Labelle

look like puzzles waiting to be deciphered. Unfortunately, only Kamba beadworkers could bring an answer to them, since written information on their art is almost non-existent.

The tendency to create evocative or figurative designs is marked among agricultural peoples who have practised basketmaking from time immemorial, and have applied their weaving techniques to beadwork. This weaving technique provides flat surfaces, often white in colour, on which contrasting designs can be made to stand out.

Some styles sometimes referred to as Eastern Zambezi,[34] which could be Yao of Tanzania and Malawi, are resolutely geometric. The very tight and regular technique of bead weaving suggests the use of a loom. Here symmetry prevails. On certain early twentieth century Yao belts (Figures 71 and 72), there is a predominance of lozenges of different colours on a background divided into square or rectangular partitions that are also coloured. These segments, and the change of lozenge colour, produce unlimited variations in visual effects. The dividing lines between the lozenges and the sections are themselves made up of three, four or more rows of contrasting colours, most often white/red or white/blue, which reinforces the stability of the design. The symmetry is sometimes perfect; in many cases, however, it is broken voluntarily, or involuntarily if there is not enough room left at the end of a belt to end the motif in an equal fashion.

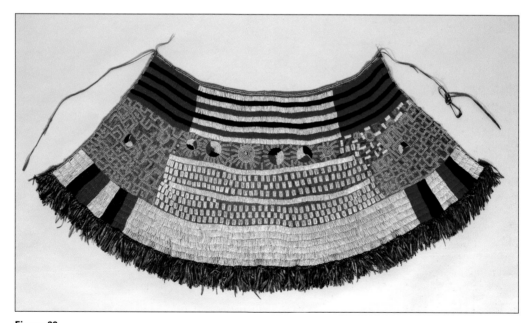

Figure 69

Skirt
Iraqw, Tanzania
Second half of the 20th century
Animal hide, glass beads, brass and plant fibre
59.5 cm (l) x 151.0 cm (w)
Royal Ontario Museum 991.238.1
With the permission of the Royal Ontario Museum © ROM

Although Zulu women made equal use of triangle and lozenge patterns, as in traditional basketry, the beaded surfaces of late nineteenth century Zulu ornaments are treated quite differently from those of the Yao for example. Many interpretations have been suggested for these shapes. In reality however, this motif could have been used for purely practical reasons: it is easily integrated onto a surface (e.g. more easily than the circle) and creates harmonious lines as well as infinite variations. Interpretations include a desire for the protection of the ancestors as when this design appeared on the shields of young men. Other interpretations suggest an "incomplete" feminine symbol (i.e. an unmarried woman) when the triangle is pointed toward the top, and a masculine symbol when pointed toward the bottom. The lozenge, or two joined triangles, would evoke a complete woman, i.e. one with children. When the points are joined (in the form of an hourglass), it would represent a complete masculine symbol (i.e. a married man).[35]

Once again, and in light of the examination of dozens of older pieces of Zulu origin, these interpretations do not hold true. It is certain that patterns of triangles and diamonds, as well as chevrons (or zigzags), stripes, crosses, circles (rarely), rectangles, squares, and earlier checkerboards express an ideal of Zulu life (recalling that many of these motifs prevail among the

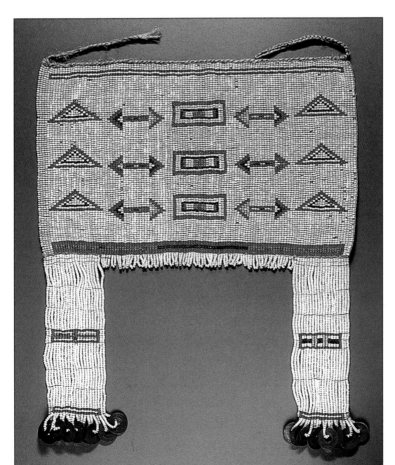

Figure 70 Kamba beadwork with its alignments of figures on a white background looks like a puzzle to be decoded.

Apron
Kamba, Kenya
Second half of the 20th century
Glass beads, plant fiber and metal coins
36 cm (l) x 31 (w) cm
Textile Museum of Canada, Toronto T94.2181
Photo: © Canadian Museum of Civilization, Steven Darby

Xhosa-speaking peoples as well). Since their origin is lost in the mists of time, their presence on these ornaments is no doubt more for purely aesthetic than symbolic reasons. The pieces on which these triangles and lozenges appeared most often were necklaces with single or multiple panels, chest ornaments ("bandoliers"), the beaded panels of skirts and belts and many ornaments worn by men and women alike. We cannot, therefore, conclude that an ornament bearing a profusion of triangles pointing toward the top would necessarily be a feminine ornament, evoking either a young girl or a married woman. By the same token, when an ornament bears several aligned lozenges, should we conclude that it evokes several married women? What would be the practical use of such an evocation? What does it mean when these triangles or lozenges are multiplied to the point of becoming mere lines separating the dominant parts of a design? In the absence of any confirmation of these meanings, it suffices to observe that each piece of beadwork represents an expression of the search for harmony

Figure 71

Belt
Yao?, Tanzania
First half of the twentieth century
Glass beads and plant fibre
73 cm (l) x 11cm (w)

Museum of Anthropology, University of British Columbia, Vancouver K4.59
Photo: © Canadian Museum of Civilization, Steven Darby

Figure 72

Belt
Yao?, Tanzania?
First half of the 20th century
Glass beads and plant fibre
83 cm (l) x 10.3 cm (w)

Vancouver Museum FF31 (F603)
Photo: © Canadian Museum of Civilization, Steven Darby

and order, in which each decorative element plays a precise and well-established role. These decorative elements are strongly codified and are found in an identical fashion on each ornament. In addition, these decorative codes are combined differently from one ornament to another. Under such conditions, to attribute meaning to these motifs seems risky. Symmetry prevails, although from time to time we find one or two isolated beads of contrasting colour appearing like the signature of the artist. Some researchers have said that these isolated beads were intended as messages, but they might also have been placed for strictly aesthetic reasons to voluntarily break the symmetry of the design. This feature is found in all beadwork from southern and eastern Africa, and helps to give it its unique character.

Finally, the space on which the beads are worked is carefully controlled and mastered. Each motif is given its proper place according to a particular order that must be carefully defined before the work is begun. Triangles or diamonds of different sizes are placed at equal distances

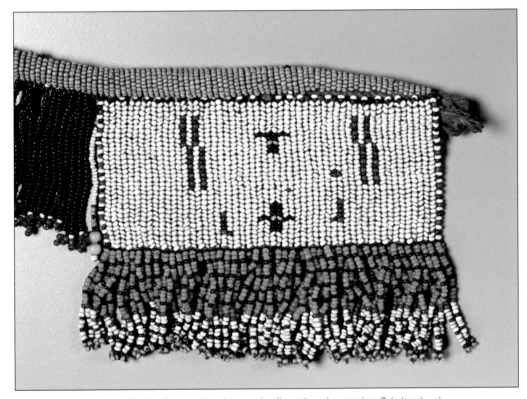

Figure 73 An evocation of familiar forms, rather than precise figuration, characterizes Zulu beadwork.

Isiheshe?
Belt (detail)
Zulu, South Africa
Late 19th or early 20th century
Glass beads and plant fibre
88 cm (l) x 12.5 cm (w)
Vancouver Museum F63 (F577)
Photo: © Canadian Museum of Civilization, Steven Darby

Figure 74 Designs in Zulu beadwork are organized according to strict guidelines, and colours are distributed with almost mathematical precision.

Ulimi
Necklace
Zulu, South Africa
Late 19th or early 20th century
Glass beads, plant fibre and brass buttons
35.3 cm (l) x 21.2 cm (w)

Textile Museum of Canada, Toronto T84.0027
Photo: © Canadian Museum of Civilization, Steven Darby

from one another while some are grouped together. Parts of the ornaments, especially in the case of chest and shoulder ornaments, include large triangles on two identical panels, while a smaller panel bears triangles or diamonds of reduced size. Symmetry is only one tool in this search for hierarchical order and is not an end in itself. In many cases, beadwork goes beyond pure symmetry and geometric forms to explore new modes of representation, leading us to think that Zulu beadwork approaches evocation. In some cases, as Sibongile Nene has remarked,[36] the predominance of the upward-pointing triangle could evoke the configuration of the huts in a traditional village against a "background" of mountains (Figure 74) or, at times, as on the belt in Figure 73, the silhouette of a cow with its horns. However, the very essence of the spirit inherent in this beadwork is a highly calculated adherence, in the use of forms and colours, to the principles of early Zulu society that included a hierarchical system of royalty and a "military" structure.

Figure 75 Symmetry, attention to detail, and refinement in the use of colours characterize Xhosa beadwork.

Isigcina or *Amatikiti*
Necklaces
Xhosa, South Africa
Second half of the 20th century
Glass beads, sinew and mother-of-pearl buttons
Top to bottom: 40.2 cm (l) x 5.7 cm (w); 37.4 cm x 5.1 cm; 41.8 cm x 4.2 cm
Photo: © Canadian Museum of Civilization, CMC-B-III-25, 27 and 24, Steven Darby, T2004-287

This type of beadwork reached its full expression just after the fall of the Zulu kingdom at the end of the nineteenth century. In the masterful organization of the beaded space, we cannot fail to notice a direct allusion to a highly regimented society (Figure 74). And if we compare this aesthetic to beadwork of the Xhosa-speaking peoples of the same period, notably the Mfengu, we can see that the spirit is very different although the latter use virtually the same motifs. The aesthetics of Xhosa beadwork are more systematic and the motifs are treated in a symmetrical fashion within the space, being more decorative than evocative.

During the twentieth century, the motifs used in Xhosa and Zulu beadwork were continuously refined, multiplied and elaborated with new colours. The space became saturated,

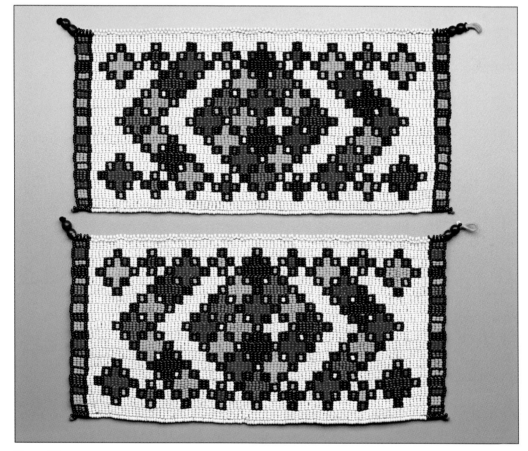

Figure 76

Idavathi
Anklets
Zulu, South Africa
Second half of the 20th century
Glass beads and plant fibre
Each: 22 cm (l) x 11 cm (w)

Museum of Anthropology, University of British Columbia, Vancouver K5.139
Photo: © Canadian Museum of Civilization, Steven Darby

Figure 77 In earlier times, only a few beads would be used to decorate clothing and adornments; today, however, beads cover the entire surface.

Bag

San, Botswana
Second half of the 20th century
Animal hide, plant fibre and glass beads
28.7 cm (l) x 25.4 cm (w)

Textile Museum of Canada, Toronto T86.0105
Photo: © Canadian Museum of Civilization, Steven Darby

losing a little of the "royal" grandeur it possessed at the end of the nineteenth century (Figures 75 and 76). The surfaces of skirts, bags and all other beaded objects tended to be filled to the point of saturation. An example is the beaded bags of the San (Figure 77). Once completely devoid of decoration, they were slowly but surely decorated with a few isolated beads, then with small clusters of beads here and there and finally, with beaded motifs covering nearly the entire surface of the leather. These motifs, similar to those seen on garments, were distributed across

Figure 78 The Yei of Botswana created a unique style of contrasting black and white, producing striking optical effects.

Apron
Yei, Botswana
Second half of the 20th century
Glass beads, sinew, animal hide and plastic button
44.2 cm (l) x 38.3 cm (w)
Photo: © Canadian Museum of Civilization, CMC-B-III-93, Steven Darby, T2004-288

Figure 79

Belt
Yei, Botswana
Second half of the 20th century
Glass beads, sinew, animal hide and ostrich eggshell
46 cm (l) x 62 cm (w)
Museum of Anthropology, University of British Columbia, Vancouver Aa1
Photo: © Canadian Museum of Civilization, Steven Darby

the surface and were formed of coloured concentric circles, rectangles, or even small unde-fined "heaps" of beads linked by additional lines of beads. These motifs, corresponding to a period marked by a considerable loss of traditional habitat among the San of Botswana, evoke isolated encampments linked together by paths. As the San have forever lost their traditional way of life and have been settled in permanent villages where they survive on government aid and crafts made for tourists, it is perhaps not surprising that their beadwork completely fills the surfaces of their leather bags, suggesting the overpopulation of the villages in which they now live and receive their aid.

Beadwork was adopted late by the San through contact with sedentary Bantu peoples, and their beadwork plays constantly with the idea of symmetry. On beaded headbands and belts, for instance, the background and the contrasting design, most often a diamond, often

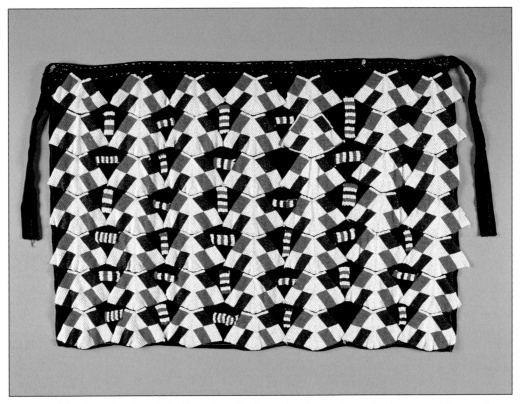

Figure 80 Although the Tonga's traditional goatskin skirts bore only a few beaded motifs, the surface of new cloth skirts is completely covered.

Sikomoka
Skirt
Tonga, Zimbabwe
Second half of the 20th century
Cloth, glass beads and plant fibre
37.8 cm (l) x 70.7 cm (w)

On loan from the William and Barbara McCann Collection
Photo: © Canadian Museum of Civilization, Steven Darby

alternate colours to produce a negative and positive version of the motif. This is also a characteristic of the Yei of the Okavango Delta, whose belts and skirts feature true optical illusions in their play between white and black (Figures 78 and 79).

The link between saturation of the beaded space and historical and economic changes is not limited to the San. It can also be seen among the Tonga of the Zambezi Valley who were displaced in a dramatic fashion from their fertile ancestral lands along the Zambezi in the late 1950s. They have gradually multiplied the pattern of the three-colour cone that decorates their fabric skirts (originally made of leather) to such an extent that it now completely fills the surface of the support, thereby creating a coloured "painting" (Figure 80). These motifs, already present on Tonga pottery, may originally have been inspired by the conical form of the straw roofs of their houses, granaries, domestic animal shelters, and their rain shrines.[37] Their accumulation alters the original motif to such an extent that it becomes unrecognizable, creating a sensation of movement and encumbrance of space that seem to evoke the drama lived by the Tonga during this period.

During the conflicts of the late nineteenth century, and later as a result of the introduction of apartheid, the Transvaal Ndebele suffered considerably from the loss of their ancestral lands and are undoubtedly the only group to have pushed representation in beadwork to this extent. It appears that they enshrined the suffering of permanent exile in the motifs featured on the

Figure 81 White once predominated in Ndebele adornments. South Africa, early 20th century.

Photo: Duggan-Cronin Collection, McGregor Museum, Kimberley

different skirts worn by females of all ages. The first known versions of Ndebele beadwork contained only a few motifs (Figure 81). The omnipresent white background was only occasionally punctuated with points of colour which often resemble letters of the Roman alphabet.

At the end of the first half of the twentieth century, with their identity threatened, Ndebele women began to paint their houses and yard walls in coloured geometric motifs. They naturally transferred these motifs to their beadwork. During the final decades of the twentieth century, the white background had completely disappeared in favour of colour (Figure 82). It is noteworthy as well that the coloured designs are applied as if with a brush in straight, long bands often shaded with black, giving them an appearance very close to that of wall paintings (Figure 83).

In addition to purely geometric designs, many figurative designs are representations of houses, yards and architectural elements, stairs, roofs, gables, fences, and other objects from the surrounding environment such as aeroplanes and electric bulbs. Indeed, the configuration of certain aprons resembles architectural drawings, depicting in particular the entrance of the house and the square shape of the yard, and perhaps even the placement of the rooms. This type of representation stakes a sort of claim, extolling the stability of the house, the last bastion of the Ndebele.

Beadwork techniques vary from north to south. Once obtained locally, the threads used for beadwork were goat or cow sinew, or threads of plant fibre (sisal), the rigidity of which made sewing relatively easy. In the twentieth century, cotton thread made its appearance, particularly in South Africa, necessitating the use of needles. Today, it is sometimes replaced

Figure 82

Liphotu
Apron
Ndebele, South Africa
Second half of the 20th century
Cloth, glass beads and plant fibre
51.5 cm (l) x 43.8 cm (w)

Museum of Anthropology, University
of British Columbia, Vancouver Ab342
Photo: © Canadian Museum of
Civilization, Steven Darby

with nylon thread. In other regions, notably in East Africa, women sometimes recycle synthetic thread from grain bags.

The beadwork techniques used in eastern and southern Africa derive directly from ancestral techniques adapted to local materials. Ornaments originally woven from fibres, were succeeded by woven beadwork. The fibre fringes of skirts and ornaments were replaced with fringes of beads (or they sometimes appeared simultaneously, as on the *inkciyo* skirt of the Xhosa). In the past, items of clothing or jewellery consisted of a piece of leather decorated with several cowries or metal beads; their modern equivalents use glass beads on leather, with the beads taking on greater importance over the years. Ornaments of thick metal wire that encircled the limbs and the neck have been replaced by new versions using metal or fibre thread as a base material onto which beads are threaded. As often seen among the Maasai of Kenya and Tanzania, the beads encircle the skin (arms, wrists, ankles) directly, imitating the original metallic coils.

The most simple beading technique is threading. It is used by everyone, from the Dinka of the southern Sudan to the Xhosa of South Africa. Another common technique is the coiling of rows of beads about a circular support that was once made by compressing fabric or grasses and has now been replaced in many cases with circles of rubber or recycled plastic. Used as necklaces, headbands, anklets, etc., these may be modern equivalents of ornaments of thick metal wire or grass. Beads are also frequently coiled around an object such as a wooden staff or various kinds of containers such as gourds.

Figure 83 Ndebele woman and child painting a wall. Ndebele Foundation's Cultural Centre for Women and Youth, South Africa.

Photo: M. Courtney-Clarke

In southern Africa in particular, beads are literally "woven" together. There are many variations, from the "weaving" of beads in a brick stitch (Zulu beadwork, Figure 84), to the netting technique in which "holes" appear, creating a "net" of beads (Xhosa beadwork). The people of the Eastern Zambezi region are known for their remarkable netting technique (Figure 85). This technique can be found on the aprons of the Yao of Tanzania and Malawi. As already noted, some peoples would have used rudimentary looms to create certain tightly woven works (Figure 86). The Ndebele are known for their weaving in "chevrons," or a herringbone pattern, in which the beads form 45-degree angles. In most bead weaving, the beads are passed over and under on several different threads, ensuring a long-lasting rigidity for clothing and other adornments.[38]

Two techniques exist for sewing beads onto leather: the "lazy stitch" practised mainly by the Ndebele (Figure 87), in which the beads are sewn in parallel rows, and the "appliqué stitch,"

Figure 84 Brick stitch.

Ulimi (detail)
Necklace
Zulu, South Africa
Late 19th or early 20th century
Glass beads, plant fibre and brass buttons
31cm (l) x 21 cm (w)
Vancouver Museum F984 (FE517)
Photo: © Canadian Museum of Civilization, Steven Darby

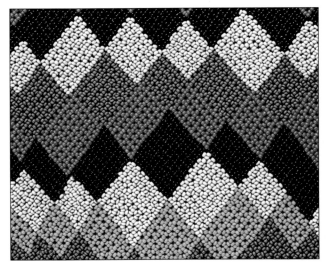

Figure 85 Three-bead netting.

Apron (detail)
Ndau or Shangaan, Zimbabwe or South Africa
First half of the 20th century
Glass beads and plant fibre
23.8 cm (l) x 17.7 cm (w)
Provincial Museum of Alberta, Edmonton H96.55.37
Photo: © Canadian Museum of Civilization, Steven Darby

in which a row of beads is sewn onto the leather and a thread is then passed between every two or three beads in order to ensure that they are solidly attached (Figure 88). Pastoral peoples of eastern Africa used this technique to embroider their leather garments and ornaments. On objects created for the tourist trade, beads are secured at much greater intervals to save time.

Finally, regarding the creation of designs of ever-expanding complexity, it is worth noting that the great precision required in beadwork could not have been obtained without the meticulous counting of beads and careful planning of the overall design. Beadworkers accomplished this without the help of a written plan.

Figure 86 Loom-weaving.

Belt (detail)
Yao?, Tanzania?
First half of the 20th century
Glass beads and plant fibre
83 cm (l) x 10.3 cm (w)
Vancouver Museum FF31 (F603)
Photo: © Canadian Museum of Civilization, Steven Darby

Figure 87 Lazy stitch.

Ijogolo (detail)
Apron
Ndebele, South Africa
Second half of the 20th century
Goatskin, glass beads, animal hair and brass
74 cm (l) x 53 cm (w)
On loan from Knight Galleries International, Toronto PSF5
Photo: © Canadian Museum of Civilization, Steven Darby

Figure 88 Appliqué stitch.

Necklace (detail)
Arsi Oromo, Ethiopia
Second half of the 20th century
Glass beads, plastic buttons, animal hide, metal, cowries and plant fibre
41 cm (l) x 32 cm (w)
Anthropology Department, Université de Montréal 61.257
Photo: © Canadian Museum of Civilization, Steven Darby

Figure 89
Ndebele woman doing beadwork.
South Africa, 1990s.
Photo: Mark Lewis

Endnotes

1. Pastoureau, 2000.
2. See especially A. Jacobson-Widding, *Red-White-Black as a Mode of Thought: A Study of Triadic Classification by Colours in the Ritual Symbolism and Cognitive Thought of the Peoples of the Lower Congo* (Uppsala: Almqvist & Wiksell, 1979).
3. He also notes that "The nursing mother applies white clay to … (her) necklaces as well as to her face to indicate that sexual relations with her husband are prohibited during this period since she may not conceive until the baby is weaned as this would endanger its life." Costello, 1990.
4. Boram-Hays, p. 174.
5. Costello, 1990.
6. Axel-Ivar Berglund: "Red, the colour of blood and frequently related to menstruation and pregnancy, as a symbol, plays an important role in fertility and pregnancy." p. 356
7. Carol S. Boram-Hays, p. 176. "*Sangomas* wear the *amagalantiya*, the kind of actually red-white string of beads around the neck and around the wrists and ankles. And the reason for that is basically for protection of the joints or of those areas." Sibongile Nene, Research Assistant/ Consultant for the Zulu section of the **Beads of Life** exhibition, interviewed on December 10, 2003 in Toronto.

8. Victor Turner, *The Forest of Symbols: Aspects of Ndembu Ritual* (Cornell University Press, New York, 1967), pp. 82-83.

9. Kuwee Kumsa, interviewed on April 25, 2003 at the Canadian Museum of Civilization.

10. Kassam, 1988, p. 14.

11. Ibid.

12. Gerhard Lindblom, *The Akamba in British East Africa: An Ethnological Monograph* (New York: Negro Universities Press, 1969), (1920 or. ed.).

13. Ingo R. Lambrecht, "Cultural Artefacts and the Oracular Trance States of the Sangoma in South Africa," in *Art and Oracle: African Art and Rituals of Divination*, New York: Metropolitan Museum of Art, 2002.

14. Eileen Jensen Krige, *Social System of the Zulus* (Pietermaritzburg: Shuter and Shooter, 1936).

15. Berglund, 1989.

16. Gary N. Van Wyk, "Illuminated Signs: Style and Meaning in the Beadwork of the Xhosa- and Zulu-Speaking Peoples," *African Arts*, vol. 36(3) (Los Angeles: UCLA, 2003).

17. Pastoureau: "A colour never 'arrives' alone, it does not take its meaning, it does not 'function' fully except when it is associated with, or placed in contrast with, one or several others."

18. Kassam, 1988.

19. See Chapter 5.

20. A colour test undertaken among Maasai women revealed the extreme rigidity of colour associations in beadwork. Labelle, Fieldwork, 1984–1985.

21. Notion raised by Donna Klumpp, 1987.

22. Marja-Liisa Swantz, *Ritual and Symbol in Transitional Zaramo Society, with Special Reference to Women*, Studia Missionalia Upsaliensia XVI, Gleerup, 1970, "The Organic Colour Scheme," p. 241.

23. Tom Phillips, ed., *Africa, the Art of a Continent* (New York: Prestel, 1995).

24. Robert J. Thornton, *Space, Time and Culture among the Iraqw of Tanzania* (New York: Academic Press, 1980).

25. Ibid., 1980, pp. 94-95.

26. Ngubane, "Body and Mind" quoted by Ingo R. Lambrecht, Cultural Artifacts.

27. Labelle, Fieldwork, 1984–1985.

28. Thornton, 1980.

29. Ibid.

30. The skirt in the Royal Ontario Museum was not available for the **Beads of Life** exhibition and was replaced by a skirt of older manufacture from the Indianapolis Museum of Art.

31. It explains why some skirts, particularly the older ones, are devoid of beads on the spots which are hidden when the skirt is worn.

32. See Chapter 6.

33. C.W. Hobley, *A-Kamba and other East African Tribes* (London: Frank Cass and Co Ltd., 1910).

34. Michael Stevenson and Michael Graham-Stewart, *South East African Beadwork, 1859-1910: From Adornment to Artifact to Art* (Fernwood Press, 2000).

35. Alice Mertens, H.S. Schoeman, *The Zulu* (Cape Town: Purnell, 1975).

36. Nene, 2003.

37. An idea inspired by the sketches of Barrie Reynolds, *The Material Culture of the Peoples of the Gwembe Valley*, Kariba Studies, Vol. III (Manchester University Press, 1968), fig. 1–6, pp. 14–25, and confirmed by Bibiana Nalwiindi Seaborn in an interview given on October 24, 2003 at the Canadian Museum of Civilization.

38. Information from Caroline Marchand, conservator at the Canadian Museum of Civilization for beaded artifacts featured in the exhibition **Beads of Life**.

STATUS CLOTHING AND ORNAMENTS

5

Throughout the cycle of life in eastern and southern Africa, with the help of body painting, hairstyles, scarring and markings, ornaments and clothing, an individual's appearance was constantly modified, like a sculpture that could be continually improved in contour, form and size. From birth to death, materials and objects transformed the socially "undefined" newborn into a fully social being whose physical appearance bore witness to participation in a private or public ritual, a completed stage in its social evolution, or a personal accomplishment. It would be impossible within the scope of this book to undertake an inventory of all the beaded ornaments, clothing and personal objects that indicated social status in eastern and southern Africa in the past and that continue to do so today. Instead, we must limit ourselves to several examples, focusing on objects in Canadian collections.

The most important stages in life marked by the wearing of specific ornaments were infancy, initiation, marriage, motherhood, fatherhood, maturity and power. While feminine adornments tended to indicate marriage, motherhood and ties to the masculine universe (husbands and sons), most of the masculine adornments attested to the acquisition of different stages in maturity, providing the wearer with access to "speech," wisdom and power.

Throughout eastern and southern Africa, birth was accompanied by celebrations involving close relatives, neighbours, and even the wider community. At the moment of birth itself, specific ceremonies such as the ritual disposal of the umbilical cord and placenta[1] were performed to symbolically ensure the newborn's survival. Subsequent rituals often included the sacrifice of an animal chosen according to the gender of the newborn, and the application of objects and materials to the body of the baby and its parents. The child would wear reminders of these past ceremonies during its first year or so.

The objects aimed at protecting the child from the evil eye, which brings illness and death, varied according to the region and culture. They included cowries, ostrich eggs, white, black or green beads, amulets, small bells, seeds, wood and many other materials.

As we have already noted, the colour white brings luck and health. Dawn Costello describes the ceremony that introduced a Xhosa baby to its ancestors. The mother smeared her child with red ochre, a goat was sacrificed and each guest received white beads from the child's father. These beads were immediately returned with the words "We thank the ancestors for their blessing." The mother then threaded the beads onto a necklace that was placed around the child's neck.[2] Among the Ndebele, a row of beads, *umucu*, was placed around the child's neck to introduce it to the group and bring it luck.[3] Among the Swazi, a row of white beads was worn around the child's waist, wrists and ankles until it was weaned.[4]

Elsewhere, other colours fulfilled the same function. Among certain Turkana clans, for example, a band of blue and black beads was placed over the child's right shoulder and under its left arm. It was removed during a ceremony held about a year later. In other cases, the baby

Figure 90 Very young children required special protection. Samburu mother, Kenya, 1990.
Photo: Marie-Louise Labelle

wore a row of black beads around its neck and another around its wrist for protection against witchcraft and sickness.[5] Green beads played the same role.

Amulets prepared by a diviner or a healer could be added to enhance protection of the child against the "evil eye." In most cases, these consisted of small leather sachets filled with beneficial herbs ground into a powder. As early as 1906, Mayr indicated that medicinal amulets in the form of fruits from the *umtungwa* tree were threaded onto a cord made of goatskin that was passed around the neck and the lower back of a Zulu child to ensure good health.[6] The gall bladder of the goat that had been ceremonially killed by the child's father might also be attached around the child's wrist.[7] The Oromo[8] and the Turkana[9] added small bells that were fixed to the baby's right wrist four days after its birth.

Figure 91 Samburu unmarried young woman. Kenya, 1990.
Photo: Marie-Louise Labelle

One of the child's first "garments" was the baby carrier, which was made in a ritual fashion. Among the Turkana, the baby carrier (*anapet*) was made from the skin of a ram or goat that was carefully chosen for its colour and sacrificed during a ceremony. To protect the child against witchcraft, small pieces of twig from a tree were attached to the baby carrier, as well as any other element believed to increase protection, such as black beads.[10] Finally, the baby was shaved, and smeared with animal fat and ochre, as he or she would be at each future transition in life. In earlier days, the Zulu also believed that red ochre and animal fat could lower a fever.[11]

If these protective agents for babies, particularly beads, cowries and beads of ostrich egg, had effectively served their purpose, they were reused later in ornaments worn either by the mother or the child. Some of them could last a lifetime, and beyond, passed down from generation to generation.

As they grew, boys and girls acquired the right to wear the clothing, ornaments, body paint and markings and hairstyles that indicated specific stages of development. In many societies, a child's earlobes were pierced around the age of seven or eight. This piercing indicated an ability to hear others, thus implying understanding and wisdom. Over time, larger and larger pieces of wood were placed in the earlobe to enlarge the hole. Ornaments indicating status could then be inserted to mark different stages in life.

Among certain groups, the years leading up to adolescence and the period of adolescence itself were marked by an amassing of adornments intended to increase the power to seduce. Boys and girls formed couples, either romantic or platonic, during numerous dances and festivities. It was a period of intense interaction, in which amorous displays and behaviours included dancing, singing and verbal sparring. Young people took great care with their appearance. Although mothers were responsible for making ornaments for their children, young girls who had learned beadwork could now offer their creations to their chosen ones. As a result, the adornments worn by boys often implied promising relationships with young girls. Among the Zulu, a string of white beads known as *ucu* (the generic term for "thread") was offered by a young girl to the young man with whom she was in love; he in turn wore it around his neck.[12] According to Schoeman, this necklace featuring several rows of white beads had the

Figure 92 This young woman's necklace indicates that she is looking for a husband. Kenya, 1977.
Photo: Cynthia Salvadori

Figure 93 A young Nubian girl wore the *rahat* until her wedding day.

Rahat
Skirt
Sudan
Early 20th century
Animal hide, plant fibre, glass beads, cowries and other shells
49.8 cm (l) x 63.3 cm (w)

Redpath Museum, Montreal 0543.01
Photo: © Canadian Museum of Civilization, Steven Darby

Figure 94 Nubian girl wearing a *rahat*.
Photo: R. Herzog, *Die Nubier*, 1957

same value as an official betrothal.[13] By contrast, among the Samburu of Kenya, it was the *moran* (initiated and unmarried young man) friend of a young girl who offered her, a few at a time, the rows of beads that she stacked around her neck, ultimately compelling her to keep her chin raised. This also indicated her loving engagement, although it could never lead to marriage.[14] (Figure 91)

Turkana girls approaching marriage wore ornaments to help possible suitors identify them from afar. They included a long, straight band of skin, decorated with beads in a pattern of contrasting colours that featured either arches or circles. It hung between the breasts, reaching below the waist in front, and fell down the back from the nape of the neck. It is very likely that this ornament was once sewn with cowries or ostrich eggshell beads. One or two necklaces composed of many rows of beads layered under the chin (reminding us of the Samburu girl's necklace mentioned above) were added to this ensemble. Additionally, at the nape of her neck, the girl wore a stiff piece of leather with three circles of beads in contrasting colours sewn on the necklace (Figure 49). These ornaments were removed after marriage, but the young girl

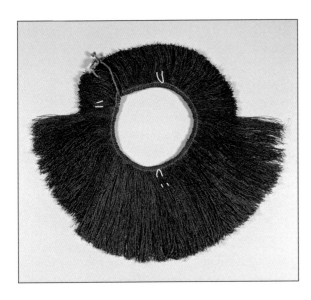

Figure 95

Manda
Skirt
Tonga, Zimbabwe
Second half of the 20th century
Plant fibre and glass beads
23.8 cm (l), 66 cm (circumference), 58 cm (diameter)
Textile Museum of Canada, Toronto T94.3015
Photo: © Canadian Museum of Civilization, Steven Darby

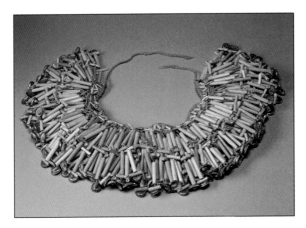

Figure 96 This skirt is a modern version of the traditional *manda* skirt that was originally made of bark fibre.

Manda
Skirt
Tonga, Zimbabwe
Second half of the 20th century
Bamboo, bottlecaps and plant fibre
31 cm (l) x 63 cm (w)
Textile Museum of Canada, Toronto T94.3019
Photo: © Canadian Museum of Civilization, Steven Darby

continued to wear them if she became a man's common-law wife and the mother of his children (Figure 92).[15] According to the photographs taken in the Turkana region at the end of the twentieth century, this necklace seems to have disappeared from use.

Depending on their age, young girls of eastern and southern Africa wore short aprons and skirts of all kinds. These were quite distinct from the garments worn by their mothers, and in earlier times were often made of plant fibre that may have enhanced fertility. The oldest of these types of skirts probably is the *rahat* of Nubian girls (Figures 93 and 94).[16] This skirt was made either of plant fibres or strips of leather and was often decorated with pendants of cowries or beads. Entirely beaded versions exist, although these may have been made for sale to foreigners. One example of a fibre skirt that existed until recently is the *manda* fibre skirt of Tonga women

Figure 97 Young Ndebele girl and her *lighabi*. Ndebele Foundation's Cultural Centre for Women and Youth, South Africa.

Photo: M. Courtney-Clarke

of the Zambezi valley, worn primarily by girls and young women (Figures 95 and 96). It was made by twisting threads of bark fibre, a long and tedious task. Bibiana Nalwiindi Seaborn, who is of Tonga origin, told us that she had seen these skirts made in the late 1980s.[17] The *lighabi*, a short apron of fibres and beads, is still worn by Ndebele girls in the villages where women sell their beadwork creations (Figure 97). Short leather aprons, including the *arach* worn by Turkana girls, have become quite rare. Made of goatskin and decorated with beads of ostrich eggshell, the *arach* was worn until marriage (Figure 26).[18]

It is probable that the short *isigege* (Figure 99) and *isiheshe* (Figure 101) skirts, which were worn by young Zulu girls and featured a beaded front panel and beaded fringes, at one time included a simple leather panel and fibre fringes. In describing the traditional dress of the Zulus, writers in the late nineteenth and early twentieth centuries actually mention grass skirts worn by young Zulu girls. The *isigege* and the *isiheshe* may be extensions of the string of beads worn around the waist by young children. For boys, this string of beads became the *umutsha* belt, the front of which was decorated with *isinene*, made of animal tails or strips of leather,

Figure 98 This ornament, a beaded version of the original *umutsha*, was probably worn by a young man.

Belt
Zulu, South Africa
Late 19th or early 20th century
Glass beads, plant fibre and brass buttons
57 cm (l) x 21.5 cm (w)

Museum of Anthropology, University of British Columbia, Vancouver K5.96
Photo: © Canadian Museum of Civilization, Steven Darby

while the back was decorated with *ibheshu*, made of a square piece of goatskin.[19] This ornament has a beaded version, as seen in Figure 98, which retains the structure of the traditional *umutsha*. Other types of *umutsha* worn by young women (Figure 100) are composed of a varying number of beaded rolls sewn together, and sometimes include one or two beaded panels. In some cases, the term *umutsha* appears to be a generic term for "belt," designating women and men's ornaments alike. Some of these ornaments have survived to the present day.

At the end of the nineteenth century, young Zulu people appear to have worn impressive quantities of beaded ornaments. Many of them wore shawls and loincloths made of fabric richly embroidered with beads, as shown in Figures 103 and 104.

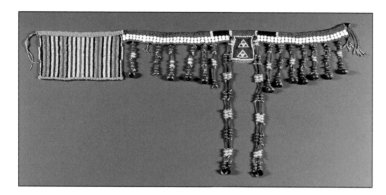

Figure 99

Isigege?
Belt
Zulu, South Africa
Late 19th or early 20th century
Glass beads, plant fibre and brass
35.6 cm (l) x 76.8 cm (w)
Redpath Museum, Montreal 05018
Photo: © Canadian Museum of Civilization, Steven Darby

Figure 100

Umutsha
Belt
Zulu, South Africa
Late 19th or early 20th century
Glass beads, plant fibre, brass buttons, metal and animal hide
87 cm (l) x 19.5 cm (w)
Glenbow Museum, Calgary FX23a
Photo: © Canadian Museum of Civilization, Steven Darby

Figure 101

Isiheshe?
Belt
Zulu, South Africa
Late 19th or early 20th century
Glass beads and plant fibre
88 cm (l) x 12.5 cm (w)
Vancouver Museum F63 (F577)
Photo: © Canadian Museum of Civilization, Steven Darby

The fertility of young girls was enhanced by the acquisition, sometimes at an early age, of dolls made by the girl's parents or even by the girl herself. These were made of clay, wood, palm nuts, straw, corncobs, bone, recycled bottles, fabric, etc. and played the role of the girl's future child. Many dolls of this kind were collected (the earliest dating from the end of the nineteenth century), no doubt because they were attractive to Westerners, particularly Western women who mistook them for toys. In reality, many of these dolls played a part in rituals and ceremonies, especially those related to initiation and marriage. They were cared for, fed and dressed like real children, and the term almost universally used for their designation means "child." Sometimes, as among the Turkana for example, if the girl gave her doll a name, she gave this name to her first-born (Figures 105 and 106). During the entire period of their initiation, Zaramo and Kwere girls of Tanzania were required to care for a wooden doll, *mwana hiti*, by feeding it, smearing it with oil, and decorating it with beads and their own hair. In the event of infertility, a young woman wore a doll on her person, carefully concealed from sight.

In southern Africa, dolls were often worn around the neck to announce a young girl's availability for marriage (Figure 107). These dolls are particularly interesting in that they show each group's ideal of beauty by preserving only the essentials of the silhouette and the most significant adornments of a wife (i.e. future mother) at the height of her beauty. Although their original use has long since disappeared, these dolls are still made, particularly for sale, because they are easily transportable and attractive to foreigners. Today however, their costumes tend to be standardized in the extreme, omitting specific details that once gave them their ritual effectiveness.

The clothing of young girls approaching marriageable age was thus very colourful and attracted a great deal of attention. At the time of initiation however, appearance underwent radical transformations among both sexes. Initiation marked the entry of boys and girls into

Figure 102

"Hlubi Youth" (detail)
South Africa, 1920s?

Photo: A.T. Bryant, *Olden Times in Zululand and Natal*, 1929.

Figure 103

Cloth
Zulu?, South Africa
Late 19th or early 20th century
Cloth, glass beads, plant fibre and brass buttons
86.6 cm (l) x 73.6 cm (w)
Vancouver Museum F44 (F415)
Photo: © Canadian Museum of Civilization, Steven Darby

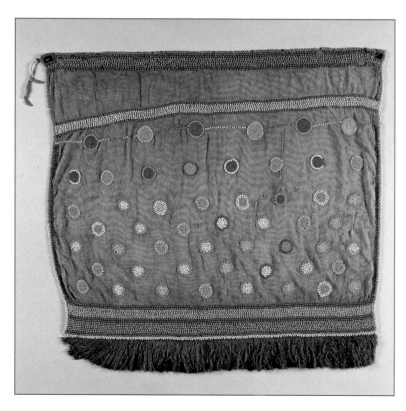

Figure 104 For the bead-worker, the horizontal alignment of fifty-two circles in contrasting colours probably evoked a familiar scene such as a landscape, a village, a group of people, or any assemblage of elements that was part of her daily life.

Cloth
Zulu?, South Africa
Late 19th or early 20th century
Cloth, glass beads, plant fibre and brass buttons
91 cm (l) x 83 cm (w)
Museum of Anthropology, University of British Columbia, Vancouver K5.101
Photo: © Canadian Museum of Civilization, Steven Darby

the society of men and women. Most of the beadwork-producing societies in eastern and southern Africa were structured into an age-set system. Within this system, all boys of approximately the same age underwent initiation together, enduring a long ceremonial process that often included physical challenges. These boys then formed an age set that gave the individual rights and duties toward the group, and remained in effect for the boy's entire lifetime. Although girls were less often divided into age sets, they were also initiated in preparation for marriage, and generally identified with groups of their male friends of the same age. A full description of the processes of initiation in eastern and southern Africa is beyond the scope of this publication. We will focus on certain particular traits related to the transformation of the body and the role of certain ornaments in this essential process.

The central characteristic of initiation was the individual's symbolic death and rebirth as a socially responsible being. Reaching this point of symbolic death required the setting aside or final rejection of the clothing and adornments of childhood and adolescence. The body,

Figure 105

Ngide
Doll
Turkana, Kenya
Second half of the 20th century
Wood, glass beads, animal hide, brass, wool, cowries,
plant fibre and pigments
52.7 cm (h) x 9.5 cm (w) x 5 cm (d)
Private collection
Photo: © Canadian Museum of Civilization, Steven Darby

Figure 106 A young
Turkana girl gave the
name of her doll to
her first child.
Kenya, 1990s.
Photo: Nigel Pavitt

thus rendered naked and unadorned by any striking or colourful ornaments, was smeared with animal fat and sometimes with white chalk. In addition, the skin or fabric clothing worn by the initiate was completely devoid of decoration, and sometimes even greased and blackened with wood charcoal. During the periods of seclusion and physical and moral testing that initiates were required to undergo, appearing in public was often forbidden and the initiate became a vulnerable body requiring protection. This explains particular body painting (often black or white) and clothing that sometimes included garments and ornaments belonging to

Figure 107

Doll Pendant
Sotho, South Africa
Late 19th or early 20th century
Cloth, glass beads, mother-of-pearl button, plant fibre
and seeds
17 cm (l), 6.5 cm (d)
Provincial Museum of Alberta, Edmonton H96.55.77
Photo: © Canadian Museum of Civilization, Steven Darby

Figure 108

Doll
Tonga, Zambia
Second half of the 20th century
Wild orange bark, resin, seeds, glass beads, plant fibre,
cloth and pigment
21 cm (l), 8 cm (d)
Glenbow Museum, Calgary R383.2
Photo: © Canadian Museum of Civilization, Steven Darby

the initiate's mother. Maasai initiates temporarily wore their mother's brass *isurutia* earrings, and Samburu initiates wore their equivalent, the *urraur* (Figure 113). Samburu and Maasai initiates wore protective elements that included natural materials such as a sisal headband, cowries and feathers, as well as dark blue, green and white beads. Such beads, called *nchipi* by the Samburu, were lent to initiates by their mothers.

All the beadwork previously worn by Xhosa youngsters was replaced with natural materials, principally plant and animal, and the body was smeared with white clay to preserve the protection

Figure 109 Young Tsonga girls made their dolls during initiation ceremonies and kept them in their homes after they were married.

Nwana
Doll
Tsonga, South Africa
Second half of the 20th century
Cloth, glass beads, plant fibre, mother-of-pearl buttons, plastic, metal and wood
17.6 cm (h) x 19.3 cm (w) x 18.8 cm (d)
Photo: © Canadian Museum of Civilization, CMC-2003.199.2, Steven Darby, T2004-289

Figure 110

Umndwana
Doll
Ndebele, South Africa
Second half of the 20th century
Glass beads, cloth, animal hide, wood and plant fibre
19 cm (h) x 9.8 cm (w) x 10.8 cm (d)
Photo: © Canadian Museum of Civilization, CMC-2003.199.4, Steven Darby, T2004-290

of the ancestors. Like Maasai and Samburu initiates, Xhosa initiates included birds and sometimes even small mammals in their hair. The blankets (made of sheepskins in the past) worn
in seclusion were burned when the initiate emerged, and they received new blankets. Among
certain Xhosa-speaking groups such as the Mfengu, these new blankets were abundantly
decorated with mother-of-pearl buttons.[20] With this emergence from seclusion, the young
people became the *abafana*, young initiates, and were now allowed to wear certain specific
adornments that set them apart during dances and ceremonies (Figures 114 to 118).

In several regions, the seclusion of initiates gave them an opportunity not only to receive
instruction about their upcoming role as adults, but also to build their future appearance. For
example, the Iraqw female initiate transformed the ritual *marmo* skirt from a simple skin cape
to the flamboyant beaded skirt of a future wife and mother. Among the Yao or other peoples
of the region, it could also take the form of a simple beaded apron (Figures 119 and 120).

During their initiation, young Xhosa girls made the *inkciyo*, a short skirt with fibre
fringes (Figure 121). During the twentieth century, the earlier brass discs encircling the leather
straps of the *inkciyo* were replaced by straps of green and yellow beads, colours that are said to
induce fertility.[21]

Figure 111

Udoli
Doll
Zulu, South Africa
Second half of the 20th century
Cloth, glass beads and plant fibre
13.8 cm (h) x 7.8 cm (w) x 8.6 cm (d)
Photo: © Canadian Museum of Civilization, CMC-2003.199.3,
Steven Darby, T2004-291

Figure 112 Ndebele girl. South Africa, 1990s.
Photo: Mark Lewis

For their daughters' initiation, the Ndebele women of the Transvaal made the stiff *isiphephetu* apron (Figure 122). A rectangle of leather once decorated with white beads, today it is richly coloured and bears depictions of houses and modern elements representing the mother's wishes for her daughter's future life.[22]

Emergence from seclusion symbolized rebirth. Initiates were bathed to erase all evidence of the initiation's stages. They were then shaved, smeared with red ochre and animal fat to restore a social appearance to the body, and adorned, either with the initiate's previous ornaments, to which new ones had been added, or a completely new set of ornaments. For girls, the period that followed represented the approach to marriage. Boys had now earned the right to participate in activities specific to their new status: most of these activities were aimed at teaching them the rights and duties linked to their age set. The Maasai and Samburu *morans*

Figure 113 Samburu initiate with his mother's *urraur* earrings, temporarily hung from a necklace of blue beads that refer to God. Kenya, 1990. Photo: Marie-Louise Labelle

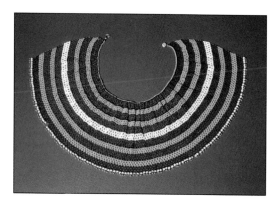

Figure 114 The white band of beads may indicate that the young man who wore it had been accepted as the friend of a young girl.

Icangci
Necklace
Xhosa, South Africa
Second half of the 20th century
Glass beads, sinew and mother-of-pearl button
17.8 cm (l) x 52.6 cm (w)

Photo: © Canadian Museum of Civilization, CMC-B-III-41, Steven Darby, T2004-292

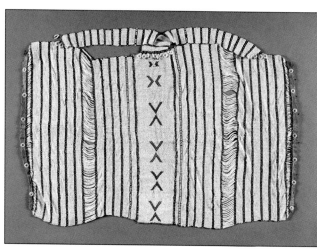

Figure 115

Ukotso
Waistcoat
Xhosa, South Africa
Second half of the 20th century
Glass beads, animal hide, iron, mother-of-pearl buttons and sinew
52.7 cm (l)
x 41.8 cm (w)

Photo: © Canadian Museum of Civilization, CMC-B-III-45, Steven Darby, T2004-293

Figure 116

Ingxowa
Bag
Xhosa, South Africa
Second half of the 20th century
Cloth, glass beads, plant fibre, plastic buttons and safety pins
32 cm (l) x 29 cm (w)

Photo: © Canadian Museum of Civilization, CMC-B-III-66, Steven Darby, T2004-294

(initiated young men) underwent several years of teaching during which their bodies and long hair were elaborately adorned (Figure 123). The adoption of beads and cotton fabrics (usually dyed with red ochre) dramatically increased the decorative aspect of this traditional dress, at the expense of the metal ornaments and leather garments of earlier times that had been designed to demonstrate personal qualities and accomplishments (Figure 124).

The Dinka of the southern Sudan wore beaded ornaments specifically linked to their age-set system. These included the beaded male corset and the corresponding female vest. These ornaments were developed over the course of the twentieth century as beads became available

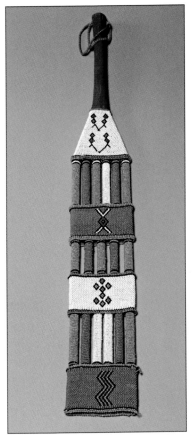

Figure 117 Young Xhosa men carried sticks such as these during dances.

Ivoti
Staff
Xhosa, South Africa
Second half of the 20th century
Wood, plant fibre and glass beads
74.9 cm (l) x 10.2 cm (w)
Photo: © Canadian Museum of Civilization, CMC-B-III-8, Steven Darby, T2004-295

Figure 118 Two young initiated Xhosa men on their way to a dance. South Africa, 1960s.
Photo: Alice Mertens. *African Elegance*, 1973

in vast quantities. Although mostly worn by the Bor, a section of the Dinka, they have since acquired the status of an identifying emblem among Dinka refugees affected by war and genocide.

A boy between the ages of sixteen and eighteen officially marked his entry into the age-set system by facial scarring. Through rituals that included isolation in special villages, as well as ceremonies and dances, young boys earned the right to wear ornaments such as bracelets of ivory and beaded ornaments, including beaded corsets. Girls, who were also divided into age sets and participated in the activities of the corresponding male groups, wore beaded vests.

Figure 119 This apron was probably worn by an initiated girl.

Apron
Yao?, Tanzania?, Malawi?
First half of the 20th century
Glass beads and plant fibre
41 cm (l) x 52.6 cm (w)
Provincial Museum of Alberta, Edmonton H96.55.42
Photo: © Canadian Museum of Civilization, Steven Darby

Each of the colours in these corsets and vests indicated a particular age set. Makueng Maliet, an Agar Dinka, and Zeinab Mokwag, a Bor Dinka, have described to us the various colours of corsets and vests once worn in association with the different age sets.

For women, the first vest would be the *ngok*. Green or blue, it was worn around the age of ten or twelve. The yellow and black *goor* was worn next by girls, many of whom were already married. This was followed by the red *alual* (or *aluel*) worn by women in their late twenties (Figure 125), and finally by the black and dark blue *acol* worn by older women.

For men, the first corset was the blue *alaak*. This was followed by the red and black *malual* (or *maluel*), which was worn from fifteen to twenty-five years of age (Figure 126). Next came the pink or mauve *ayor*, worn from age twenty-five to thirty, and finally the yellow and black

Figure 120

Apron
Ndau? or Shangaan?, Zimbabwe? or
South Africa?
First half of the 20th century
Glass beads and plant fibre
23.8 cm (l) x 17.7 cm (w)
Provincial Museum of Alberta, Edmonton
H96.55.37
Photo: © Canadian Museum of Civilization,
Steven Darby

Figure 121

Inkciyo
Apron
Xhosa, South Africa
Second half of the 20th century
Glass beads, plant fibre and animal hide
16 cm (l) x 36 cm (w)
Photo: © Canadian Museum of Civilization,
CMC-B-III-53, Steven Darby, T2004-296

magor, which was worn past the age of thirty. The male corset is easily recognized by its projection supported by a metal wire which flings itself skyward at the back of the body. The Dinka call this projection "horn" (*tung*), perhaps in reference to their cows' horns.[23] It is probable that these beaded corsets and vests were simple belts and necklaces at one time, as seen in the photo of a young married Dinka woman taken during the first half of the twentieth century (Figure 5).

These impressive ornaments perhaps did not have as much importance or value among the Dinka as the marriage necklace. This necklace was made of several rows of antique blue Venetian beads enhanced in the centre with large white beads and black beads with white dots (these last two were called *matuelder*). The future groom was required to wear this necklace

Figure 122 On the apron of a young female initiate, her mother would embroider what she wished for her daughter — in this case, a house.

Isiphephetu
Apron
Ndebele, South Africa
Second half of the 20th century
Cloth, glass beads and plant fibre
28.8 cm (l) x 36.2 cm (w)

Museum of Anthropology, University of British Columbia, Vancouver ab347
Photo: © Canadian Museum of Civilization, Steven Darby

Figure 123

Enkimeita (detail)
Belt
Maasai, Kenya
Second half of the
20th century
Animal hide, glass
beads, metal and
plastic buttons
79 cm (l) x 12.5 cm (h)
Private collection
Photo: © Canadian
Museum of Civilization,
Steven Darby

Figure 124 Maasai *moran* with his belt and bracelet. Throughout the twentieth century, the physical appearance of Maasai and Samburu *morans* made them objects of fascination to tourists. Kenya, 1985.

Photo: Marie-Louise Labelle

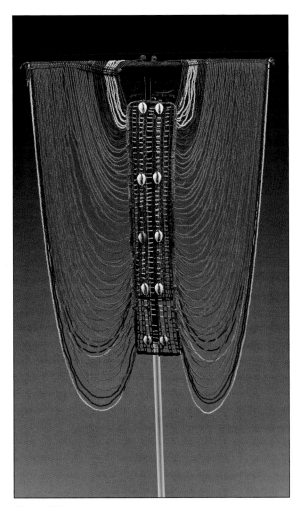

Figure 125

Aluaŋ
Woman's Vest
Dinka, Sudan
Second half of the 20th century
Glass beads, cowries, plant fibre, iron, cloth and animal hide
62.5 cm (l) x 37.5 cm (w)

Photo: © Canadian Museum of Civilization, CMC-2002.20.1,
Steven Darby, T2004-297

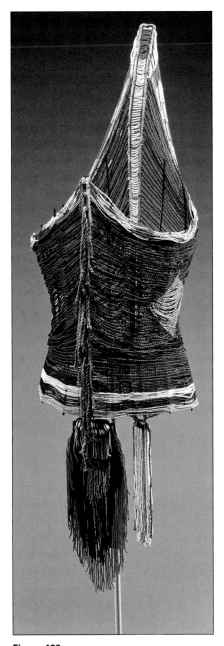

Figure 126

Maluaŋ
Male Corset
Dinka, Sudan
Second half of the 20th century
Glass beads, cowries, plant fibre, cloth and iron
90.6 cm (l) x 46.5 cm (w)

Photo: © Canadian Museum of Civilization,
CMC-2002.20.2-a/b, Steven Darby, T2004-298

before marriage. Once married, he would give it to his wife, who would wear it for a period of time. According to Makueng Maliet and Zeinab Mokwag,[24] when the young woman became pregnant, she would remove a large portion of the necklace from her neck and keep only one or two rows from it. She would then return the necklace to those from whom it was borrowed. This necklace, which was considered to be of very great value, was simply named "the beads of the Bor" or "the beads of the Agar," depending on the Dinka group to which it belonged. Once passed down from generation to generation, these beads are no longer available in local markets.[25]

In most societies of eastern and southern Africa, marriage led to radical changes of costume. As she prepared for marriage either in her mother's village or upon her arrival in her husband's village, the young woman donned new clothes such as skirts and capes which not only made her easy to identify but also covered parts of the body that were previously put on display. It was crucial to be able to distinguish the silhouette of a married woman from that of a young girl, even from a distance, to ensure that proper behaviour could be adopted when encountering her (Figure 127). This distinction could be accentuated, if need be, by the rustling of the woman's skirts on the ground (the *abuo* skirt of Turkana women) or even the jingling of certain pieces of jewellery.[26]

One of the most dramatic examples of this change of costume is undoubtedly that of young Turkana brides who, upon arriving in their husbands' villages, were required to remove all their old garments and put on entirely new clothing. The new clothes were made of animal skins from her husband's or in-laws' herds, and thus had a profound symbolic value, particularly as a blessing for future motherhood. The frontal *akodat* apron (Figure 128),[27] heavily decorated in red, black (or blue) and white beads, was replaced after the birth of a first child with a smaller and more severe version, the *adwel* (Figure 33) that was decorated with metal beads. The type of metal used provided a precise indication of the generation to which her husband belonged: copper, if he was of the Leopard generation; iron, lead or aluminum if he was of the Stone generation, as indicated by the metal ring (*alagama*) worn around her neck. The voluminous *abuo* back skirt (Figure 129), made from skins of goats sacrificed for that purpose, reached to the ground. The lower part of the skirt was jagged and weighted down with the flaps cut from the legs of an ox sacrificed during the marriage ceremony.[28]

From the southern Sudan to the Cape, the different skirts worn by married women have many points in common. Made either of several skins joined together, or of very thick cotton, they are of considerable weight. The intent is to cover the woman's body, thus symbolically protecting her future offspring. Among the Maasai and the Samburu, the goatskin *olokesena* skirt that was a distinctive mark of married women but is rapidly disappearing from use was characterized by several cut-outs on its lower portion. These cut-outs, which the Samburu call *icholo*, were a means of distinguishing married women from young girls who wore skirts without cut-outs (Figure 130). The cut-outs were seen as well on the *adwel* apron and the *abuo* skirt of Turkana women and on the skin cape worn in the past by Arsi Oromo women (Figures 131 and 132). They might have indicated a woman's ability to bear children and assume responsibility for her household.

All these skirts and capes once were decorated with cowries or metal beads that have since been replaced with glass beads. Today, these garments continue to play a significant role

Figure 127 The *abuo* skirt indicates that this woman is married; the *adwel* apron, with its metal beads, shows that she is a mother. Her frontal apron may indicate that she is pregnant. Kenya, 1990s.

Photo: Nigel Pavitt

in ceremonies, underlining the role of women as important members of a society and symbolizing their power. They are no longer worn on a daily basis, however, having been replaced with cotton clothing.

In South Africa, also, married women were distinguished by their clothing. The Ndebele women of the Transvaal developed a codified system of adornment, enabling the differentiation of young girls, initiated girls, married women and mothers. This codification was enhanced during the twentieth century when the wearing of traditional costume took on a new significance among the Ndebele, who were facing the loss of their ancestral lands. Following the *lighabi* (Figure 97) of young girls and the *isiphephetu* (Figure 122) of initiated girls, two beaded goatskin skirts (the skin has been replaced today with fabric) were worn to mark different stages of marriage. Both bore the cut-outs described above. These are the *liphotu* (Figure 133) and the *ijogolo* (Figure 134). The *liphotu* was worn during the wedding ceremony, and the *ijogolo* symbolized the achievement of motherhood. Various suggestions have been advanced about the particular form of these two aprons and their relationship to marriage and maternity. On its lower portion, the *liphotu* bears two lateral panels framing beaded fringes that

Figure 128

Akodat or Esiya Apron
Turkana, Kenya
Second half of the 20th century
Goatskin, glass beads and plant fibre
55.3 cm (l) x 30.3 cm (w)
Textile Museum of Canada, Toronto T87.0341
Photo: © Canadian Museum of Civilization, Steven Darby

Figure 129 The four flaps on the lower portions of this skirt were cut from the leg skin of an ox sacrificed on the wearer's wedding day.

Abuo
Skirt
Turkana, Kenya
Second half of the 20th century
Animal hide, glass beads, iron and plant fibre
128 cm (l) x 104 cm (w)

Glenbow Museum, Calgary FF 123
Photo: © Canadian Museum of Civilization, Steven Darby

were once strips of leather. It is said that these panels represent the wife and her husband, and the central fringes, the children to come. The *ijogolo* has five panels on its lower portion; the central panel might represent the mother and the panels on either side, any existing children. This skirt was worn as an emblem of motherhood, particularly during important ceremonies, while the *liphotu* skirt was worn daily. Married women wore other garments linked to their status such as the *nguba* blanket on which bands of beads are sewn (as on the *isikoti* cape worn by married Zulu women) or the *nyoka* beaded train that reaches to the ground.

Xhosa women once wore a large leather skirt, the *isikhaka*, which was replaced by the *umbhaco* (Figure 135). The *umbhaco* skirt has multiple pleats made from a panel of very thick cotton fabric, *ibhayi*, smeared with red ochre and decorated with bands of black fabric machine-sewn by local seamstresses. This skirt is an essential element in the costume of Xhosa women to the present day, when it is worn on important ceremonial occasions (Figure 136).

Added to the *umbhaco* was a piece of cotton cloth, the *incebeta*, which covered the chest and reached to the knees. Once brought to her husband's village, the bride was required to cover her head with black fabric that completely masked her face. This piece of black fabric was worn during the first months of marriage. Later, after the young woman had given birth

Figure 130 The skirts of young Samburu girls were differentiated from those of married women by their unnotched hemlines.

Nkila
Skirt
Samburu, Kenya
Second half of the
20th century
Goatskin, plant fibre and
glass beads
98.6cm (l) x approximately
72 cm (w)

Anthropology Museum,
University of Winnipeg E2A-20
Photo: © Canadian Museum of
Civilization, Steven Darby

Figure 131

Cape
Arsi Oromo, Ethiopia
Second half of the 20th century
Animal hide, glass beads, aluminum
and plant fibre
98.5 cm (l) x 78.5 cm (w)

Anthropology Department, Université
de Montréal 61.260
Photo: © Canadian Museum of
Civilization, Steven Darby

Figure 132 The skin garments once worn by Oromo women have now disappeared in favour of cloth versions.
Ethiopia, 1967.
Photo: Virginia Luling

to her first child, it was replaced with a multicoloured felt turban that was often decorated with coloured thread, beads, or mother-of-pearl buttons. In the past, this headdress was made of leather decorated with black and white beads (*umnqwazi*).

One of the most important garments worn by married Zulu women was the *isidwaba* ("ox skin") skirt, cut from the skin of a goat or an ox and smeared with wood charcoal. It was worn from the moment a young girl was engaged and therefore dictated the specific type of behaviour that was required around her. The leather *ingcayi* apron was added to this skirt, thus concealing the entire front of the body. This apron was decorated with brass studs and beads, and it had to be worn from the time of marriage until the birth of the first child, and for each subsequent pregnancy. This garment thus played an important role protecting a woman's fertility. Motherhood was indicated as well by the wearing of the *isibhamba* belt (Figure 137) which was made of interwoven grasses decorated at several points by transverse bands of beads. This belt, which supported the abdomen, could only be worn after the birth of a child. The *ixhama* or *isifociya* (Figure 10) is a wider belt made of stiff, tightly braided fibres. Earlier versions of these belts were decorated with brass studs and later with beads.[29]

In previous times, jewellery, which was often modest in size and generally made of metal, indicated marriage. Among the Maasai and the Samburu, marriage was indicated by an iron chain suspended from the ear: the *emonyorit* and the *nkaiwueli*. Spirals of brass or iron, *isurutia*,

Figure 133

Liphotu
Apron
Ndebele, South Africa
Second half of the
20th century
Goatskin, glass beads,
cloth and plant fibre
51 cm (l) x 56 cm (w)

On loan from Knight
Galleries International,
Toronto PSH15
Photo: © Canadian
Museum of Civilization,
Steven Darby

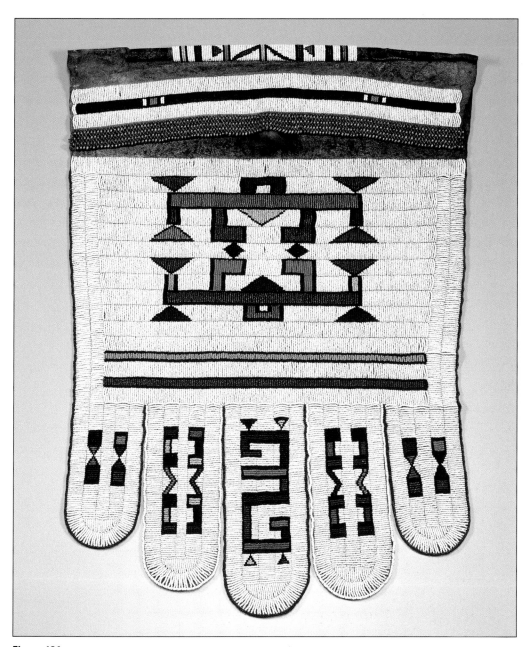

Figure 134

Ijogolo
Apron
Ndebele, South Africa
Second half of the 20th century
Goatskin, glass beads, animal hairs and brass
74 cm (l) x 53 cm (w)

On loan from Knight Galleries International, Toronto PSF5
Photo: © Canadian Museum of Civilization, Steven Darby

also played this role (Figure 138). The wearing of these ornaments was obligatory, and their loss could mean punishment by the women's husbands.[30] During the second half of the twentieth century, Maasai women's *isurutia* were gradually replaced by the *ilgoreta*, disks of leather embroidered with beads. By that time, the *isurutia* were worn only by the mothers of *morans*, and often only during ceremonies.

The Samburu and Maasai *isurutia* were once hung from two narrow bands of leather (*inchonito inkiyiaa*, Figure 139) passed through the enlarged openings of the earlobes. These bands of leather were worn as a sign of initiation and later throughout the marriage. Originally devoid of decoration, they were subsequently decorated with cowries, and then with beads until their entire surface was covered. Each band bore a different and complementary pattern.

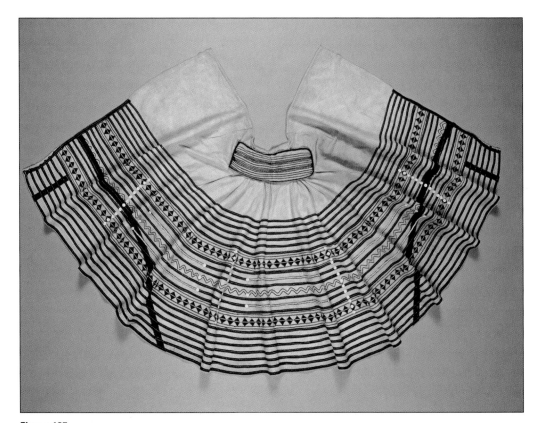

Figure 135

Umbhaco
Skirt
Xhosa, South Africa
Second half of the 20th century
Cloth, glass beads, mother-of-pearl buttons and plant fibre
87.2 cm (l) x 354 cm (w at bottom hem) x 106 cm (w at top hem)
Photo: © Canadian Museum of Civilization, CMC-B-III-68, Steven Darby, T2004-299

Figure 136 Modern interpretation of the traditional Xhosa skirt. Fashion show at the Canadian Museum of Civilization as part of "Ten Years of Freedom" celebrations in April 2004, marking the 10th anniversary of the end of apartheid. Designed by Ketso Mabusela and Angelina Ramaila.

Photo: © Canadian Museum of Civilization, Steven Darby

Another obvious sign of marriage among Samburu and Rendille women was the *mporro* (Samburu name) necklace made of plant fibres decorated with large red beads (*mporroi*) as shown in Chapter 2 (Figure 37). These mandatory necklaces were once passed down from generation to generation. Today, however, they are very quickly disappearing from use (Figure 140).

Aneesa Kassam described the metal ornaments used to indicate maternity among certain Oromo groups (see Chapter 2).[31] As previously mentioned, in several regions the initiation of a woman's son is reflected in her adornments. Beads took the place of traditional materials to indicate this event. The beads that served to protect the initiate, whether Samburu or Maasai, were carefully salvaged by his mother who wore them in long rows (Maasai: *isurri*; Samburu: *marsanten*) fastened to her *surutia* earrings. They would later be placed around the neck or limbs of her son's first-born.

The hairstyles of Zulu women clearly indicated their status (Figure 141). These included, in particular, the chignon or knot of hair in conical form known as *inhloko*; the *isicholo* hat, which was flared or cylindrical in form and made of fibres or even woven directly into the hair; hairpins made of bone and delicately decorated with animal fibres and several beads (Figure 42); and finally, the fibre or beaded *umnqwazi* headband worn on the forehead until the birth of her first child as a sign of respect toward the woman's in-laws.[32] According to Mertens, the particular colours and designs of the beadwork fastened to the base of the hat provided very precise indications on the length of the marriage, and could also indicate, for example, if the woman had given birth to children.[33]

The Ndebele wore *linga koba*, or "long tears," made of long bands of beads descending from the head (Figure 142). The *linga koba* indicated the sadness of the mother at the "loss" of

Figure 137

Isibhamba
Belt
Zulu, South Africa
Late 19th or early 20th century
Plant fibre, glass beads and animal hide
50 cm (l) x 11 cm (w)

Vancouver Museum FE361 (F581)
Photo: © Canadian Museum of Civilization, Steven Darby

Figure 138 Samburu woman with her marriage ornaments: earrings, chain and bracelet. Kenya, 1990.
Photo: Marie-Louise Labelle

Figure 139

Nchonito Nkiyiaa
Ear Flaps
Samburu, Kenya
Second half of the 20th century
Animal hide, plant fibre and glass beads
20.4 cm (l) x 5.0 cm (w)

The Consolata Missionaries, Canada HND12
Photo: © Canadian Museum of Civilization, Steven Darby

Figure 140 Singing Rendille women wearing their marriage necklaces. Kenya, 1978.
Photo: Neal Sobania

her son upon his emergence from the initiation camp, as well as her joy that he had acquired a new level of maturity. The birth of a son and his entry into the world of men were thus notable events for a woman. She not only acquired status on these occasions, but also at the next major stage in her son's life when he became a father. In the latter, certain ornaments worn at the time of his initiation were reused to protect his newborn infant. The circle was now complete.

As the years passed, mature women abandoned bright and attractive jewellery for more discreet touches such as emblems of status, or ornaments that indicated their relationships with their children. The mother took an active part in notable events within her clan. She played a role in all rites of passage for her husband, sons and daughters, and they borrowed some of her clothing and ornaments on these occasions. While the younger generation continued to create new styles of beadwork, the role of her own clothing was no longer to stand out, but

Figure 141 Modern versions of the traditional hat worn by married Zulu women. Fashion show at the Canadian Museum of Civilization as part of "Ten Years of Freedom" celebrations in April 2004, marking the 10th anniversary of the end of apartheid. Designed by Ketso Mabusela and Angelina Ramaila.

Photo: © Canadian Museum of Civilization, Steven Darby

to commemorate. The older beads she wore around her neck had a long history and stayed there until her death, "to remember," according to the words of one Samburu woman.[34]

Mature men also wore ornaments indicating status. In some regions, fatherhood, particularly of a son, was marked by the wearing of specific ornaments, especially during ceremonies. After their period of initiation had ended, mature men wore fewer ornaments in comparison to women. When they became heads of family and livestock owners, they wore discreet emblems intended to show their acquisition of maturity and wisdom. These included earrings or necklaces that were once made of metal but were later made of glass beads. Turkana men wore ostrich feathers on their heads as Booran Oromo leaders and Zulu men of importance once did.[35] Booran Oromo leaders also once wore the kalasha, a horn pointing skyward, on their heads. According to Aneesa Kassam, this ornament corresponded in form to the *benaac'u* brass disc worn by women who had borne a son. All adult Zulu males once wore the *isicoco*, a disc

Figure 142 The *linga koba* commemorates the initiation of a woman's son. Ndebele Foundation's Cultural Centre for Women and Youth, South Africa.

Photo: M. Courtney-Clarke

of braided fibres, directly in their hair. This disc, which gave them the right to marry, was evidence that the wearer had attained a certain level of maturity. The *isicoco* was the masculine equivalent of the conical chignon or the woven hat of married Zulu women. In monarchical societies such as the Zulu, or East African societies of Uganda, Rwanda and Burundi, the king and his close relatives wore numerous ornaments as emblems of royalty. These highly symbolic ornaments are still worn today during ritual celebrations.[36] During ceremonies, Maasai men who had been elected by their age set for their personal wisdom and oratorical ability wore blue capes, as did diviners and prophets when they officiated (Figure 143). Among the Oromo, iron bracelets worn on the right arm designated the leaders of each age set.

A collection of accessories and personal objects, including wooden staffs, headrests and tobacco boxes, also helped to define a man's status. These objects did not have precisely the same function in eastern and southern Africa. In eastern Africa, the wooden staff was an attribute

Figure 143 Ole Koyiaki, a Maasai prophet, recognizable by his blue and white cape, wears a snuffbox inherited from his ancestors. Kenya, 1985.

Photo: Marie-Louise Labelle

of a mature man and was sometimes in a darker colour if the owner was the spokesperson of his age set. Among the Booran Oromo, the long hororo staff was the symbol of the head of a family and of herds of livestock. Its feminine counterpart, the siiqqee, was an instrument of power for married women and is sometimes considered a symbol of solidarity and resistance to male domination (Figure 144).[37] As Aneesa Kassam has noted, a full series of wooden staffs in diverse shapes and sizes would have served throughout life to indicate the status of both men and women.[38] This is true for most of the pastoral peoples of East Africa.

Tobacco boxes, worn on a necklace of beads or chains around the neck, were used during debates among the elders, as tobacco was believed to clarify thinking (Figures 145 and 146). As for the headrest, not only did it protect a man's hairstyle but it also prevented him from sleeping so deeply that he could not remain attentive in the event of danger (Figure 148). In

Figure 144 Booran Oromo couple with their respective *siiqqee* and *hororo* marriage sticks. Ethiopia, 1995.

Photo: Van der Stappen. *Cultures et Communication*

southern Africa, most of these objects that have disappeared from daily use had religious significance. Tobacco boxes, however, are still used by diviners, as tobacco is a tool for communicating with the ancestors. It is used in divination to put the diviner in contact with the spirits (Figure 151). The *ishungu* tobacco boxes of the Zulu were heavily decorated with beads (Figures 149 and 150). The headrests also had very strong ties to the ancestors since these objects were once passed from father to son and kept in the home. They were used in divination as well, and their link to sleep, in which visions can occur, is another factor in affirming their sacred character.

Weapons of all sorts also once served as masculine attributes. These included the spears and shields of young men. The colours, forms and designs of such weapons made it possible to distinguish the exact region of origin and the age set of its owner. Ceremonial axes and clubs were worn during major ceremonies, as were knives with sheaths that had been delicately carved from wood, horn and ivory, long wooden staffs carved with human or animal figures and beaded dance staffs.

Beyond their obvious protective function, status-related ornaments, both in eastern and southern Africa, served to define precise roles within a society and thus the correct behaviour to be adopted towards each member, depending on their age and their different stages of maturity. Often mistakenly considered to be emblems of material wealth, such ornaments instead marked the personal acquisition of internal qualities.

Figure 145

Snuffbox
Kamba?, Kenya?, Tanzania?
First half of the 20th century
Bone, wood, iron, brass, aluminum and plant fibre
7.2 cm (h), 3.2 (diameter); chain 65.5 cm (l)
Museum of Anthropology, University of British Columbia, Vancouver K4.83
Photo: © Canadian Museum of Civilization, Steven Darby

Figure 146

Olkidong
Snuffbox
Maasai, Kenya
Second half of the 20th century
Wood, animal hide, glass beads, plant fibre and iron
16.6 cm (h), 3.8 (diameter)
Museum of Anthropology, University of British Columbia, Vancouver aj120
Photo: © Canadian Museum of Civilization, Steven Darby

Figure 147
Headrests
Eastern Africa
Photo: © Canadian Museum of Civilization, Steven Darby, T2004-300

From left to right:

Ekicholong
Turkana, Kenya
Second half of the 20th century
Wood, animal hide and glass beads
16.5 cm (h) x 21.2 cm (w) x 8.7 cm (d)
On loan from Nathalie Dussault

Ngecher
Pokot, Kenya
Second half of the 20th century
Wood, animal hide, glass beads and fibre
17.4 cm (h) x 11.3 cm (w) x 4.6 cm (d)
CMC-2002.22.1

Rendille, Kenya
Second half of the 20th century
Wood
7.5 cm (h) x 31.5 cm (w)
University of Alberta Art and Artifact Collection
Museums and Collections Services, Edmonton 983.57.1.20

Arsi Oromo?, Ethiopia
Second half of the 20th century
Wood, cowries, glass beads, buttons and fibre
20 cm (h) x 20 cm (w) x 14.3 cm (d)
Anthropology Department, Université de Montréal 61.328

Turkana?, Kenya
Second half of the 20th century
Wood and animal hide
21 cm (h) x 18 cm (w) x 6 cm (d)
Museums and Collections Services, Edmonton 983.57.1.5

Figure 148 Headrests, such as this one used by a Turkana man, protected men's elaborate hairstyles. Kenya, 1990s.
Photo: Nigel Pavitt

Members of a society were required to attain such qualities through their respect for the rules that had been defined by their elders and that were based on fundamental religious principles. As we shall see in the next chapter, these traditional rules of conduct have been eroded slowly but surely over the past two centuries, thus changing forever the ways in which people managed their appearance in society.

Figure 149

Snuffbox
Hlubi?, South Africa
Late 19th or early 20th century
Animal hide, blood, clay, glass beads, glass button and plant fibre
9.7 cm (h), 6.3 cm (d)
Vancouver Museum FE601
Photo: © Canadian Museum of Civilization, Steven Darby

Figure 150

Ishungu
Snuffbox
Zulu?, South Africa
Late 19th or early 20th century
Gourd, glass beads, wood and plant fibre
5.08 cm (h), 6 cm (d); beaded cord 23.4 cm (l)
Vancouver Museum FF30 (F510)
Photo: © Canadian Museum of Civilization, Steven Darby

Figure 151 Zulu *sangomas* use tobacco to communicate with their ancestors. South Africa, 2003.

Photo: Sibongile Nene, Research Assistant/Consultant for **Beads of Life** Zulu section

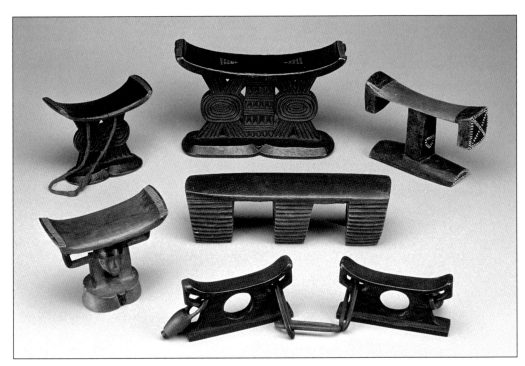

Figure 152
Headrests
Southern Africa
Photo: © Canadian Museum of Civilization, Steven Darby

Front row:

Tsonga, South Africa
Late 19th or early 20th century
Wood
8 (h) x 15 (w) x 3 (d) cm each
Redpath Museum, Montreal 06526 & 06525

Middle row, from left to right:

Tsonga, South Africa
Late 19th or early 20th century
Wood
16 (w) x 13 (h) x 5.5 cm (d)
Redpath Museum, Montreal 0373

Zulu?, South Africa
Late 19th or early 20th century
Wood
9.7 cm (h) x 30 cm (w) x 7.6 cm (d)
Redpath Museum, Montreal 0433

Back row, from left to right:

Mutsago
Shona, Zimbabwe
Late 19th or early 20th century
Wood and cloth
14 cm (h) x 17 cm (w) x 7.2 cm (d)
Redpath Museum, Montreal 04193.01

Mutsago
Shona, Zimbabwe
Late 19th or early 20th century
Wood
18 cm (h) x 28 cm (w) x 7cm (d)
Vancouver Museum FE10 (F11)

Tsonga, South Africa
Late 19th or early 20th century
Wood and glass beads
13.7 cm (h) x 20 cm (w) x 6 cm (d)
Glenbow Museum, Calgary R1915.92

Endnotes

1. Barrett, 1998.
2. Costello, 1990.
3. Ivor Powell and Mark Lewis, *Ndebele: A People and Their Art* (London: New Holland Ltd., 1995).
4. Twala, 1950.
5. Barrett, 1998.
6. Franz Mayr, "The Zulu Kafirs of Natal," *Anthropos* 1, 1906, pp. 453–71.
7. Ibid.
8. Kassam, 1989.
9. Barrett, 1998.
10. Ibid.
11. Mayr, 1906.
12. Boram-Hays, 2000.
13. H.S. Schoeman, "A Preliminary Report of Traditional Beadwork in the Mkhwanazi Area of the Mtunzini District, Zululand," *African Studies*, 27(2), 1968, pp. 57–82, 27(3), 1968, pp. 107–34.
14. Maasai and Samburu *morans* could not marry until they had passed certain stages of their education. The love affairs that developed during their time as *morans* could not concretize in marriage, which was later decided and organized by elders.
15. This trait is not uncommon for Turkana people, as the cattle price that a man has to pay for getting married is extremely high.
16. Several examples of which can be found in Canadian collections.
17. Research Assistant/Consultant for **Beads of Life**, Tonga culture, interviewed on October 24, 2003 at the Canadian Museum of Civilization.
18. See Chapter 2.
19. Krige, 1936.
20. Costello, 1990.
21. Ibid.
22. Powell, 1995.
23. All these descriptive terms are subject to verification since they depend on regional differences of language. There is also the previously noted difficulty of translating abstract colour terms using words that apply to the colours of livestock.
24. Makueng Maliet and Zeinab Mokwag, Research Assistants/Consultants for **Beads of Life**, Dinka culture, interviewed on April 4, 2003 at the Canadian Museum of Civilization.
25. Ibid.
26. The sound made by the Maasai women's *inkalulungani* (iron anklets on which pieces of metal were threaded) enabled young male initiates to hide the meat they ate to prevent the gaze of women from spoiling it.
27. Or *esiya*. The name of this apron seems to vary from one Turkana clan to another.
28. Barrett, 1998.
29. See the example in Chapter 2.
30. Labelle, 1996.
31. Kassam, 1989.
32. Krige, 1936.
33. Alice Mertens and H.S. Schoeman, *The Zulu* (Cape Town: Purnell, 1975).
34. Labelle, 1996.
35. Kassam, 1989.

36. Information gathered from Betty Kageye Kieran, Research Assistant/Consultant for **Beads of Life**, Beadwork market section, interviewed on September 30, 2003 at the Canadian Museum of Civilization.

37. Martha Kuwee Kumsa, "The Siiqqee Institution of Oromo Women," *The Journal of Oromo Studies*, vol. 4 (1-2), July 1997. Versions of these Booran Oromo staffs can be found in the collection of the Anthropology Department at the Université de Montréal.

38. Aneesa Kassam and Gemetchu Megerssa, "Sticks, Self, and Society in Booran Oromo: A Symbolic Interpretation," in *African Material Culture*, Mary Jo Arnoldi, Christraud M. Geary, and Kris L. Hardin, eds. (Indiana University Press, 1996), pp 145–166.

BEADS OF LIFE

6

From the moment Europeans started settling in eastern and southern Africa, traditional dress began to undergo drastic changes. Although most people stopped wearing their traditional clothing, those living in rural areas continued its use on a daily basis for some time. Traditional clothing continued to evolve during the twentieth century, until its near-disappearance at the dawn of the twenty-first century. In recent years, however, traditional dress has been making a comeback, albeit in a different context. For more than a century, the visual appearance, function, and of course materials of dress and ornaments, have continued to evolve, not only in response to the sometimes dramatic historical changes that their wearers experienced, but also as a result of the adoption of new ideas and fashions.

Since these changes did not happen at the same time or in the same way in all regions of eastern and southern Africa, the phenomenon is difficult to define. We will attempt to outline key periods in the evolution of functions and meanings in traditional dress, as well as the repercussions of this evolution on the continuing practice of beadwork in both eastern and southern Africa today.

The widespread introduction of European glass beads in Africa coincided with the disintegration of traditional African societies. Conflicts between settlers and local populations whose lands and possessions were coveted, coupled with forced displacements, loss of access to natural resources, and a subsequent destruction of economic systems, compelled people to abandon their villages and their ancestral way of life. Men were obliged to work in towns or on farms owned by Europeans. In order to feed themselves and gain access to European goods, they sold their livestock and other animal-related products. Trade between neighbouring peoples became less common, hunting was regulated, many blacksmiths stopped their activities, and the time once spent on the making of clothing and ornaments was given over to more immediate concerns. Materials once used became less accessible, and people began instead to acquire manufactured European materials such as glass beads and cotton fabrics that were both attractive and comfortable. Older ornaments were destroyed and the materials from which they were made — such as glass beads — were sometimes reused, or handed down until they broke or were no longer usable.

In addition, the schooling of children and religious conversions urged by Catholic and Protestant missionaries profoundly altered traditional social structures. Away from their villages, young people no longer received a traditional education, nor could they participate in important ceremonies such as those that contributed to the creation of age sets. In some cases, colonial powers even banished initiations, thus undermining the very foundations of a society.

The education of children took place in modern schools, using a language and ideas that were foreign. In addition, children were taught that traditional ways of life were a thing of the past and that the only road to salvation rested in "progress" and modernity. In order to ensure its acceptance, modern religion was cleverly presented as the logical successor to traditional

153

religions. In certain instances, missionaries forced new converts to destroy their existing cloth-ing. As for the traditional practices of healers and diviners, these were likened by colonists to witchcraft.

These profound changes began earlier in southern Africa than in eastern Africa, and more rapidly in the fertile regions coveted by the European settlers than in the semi-arid regions. The latter often remained relatively untouched, sometimes even to the present day. Once the process had begun, however, it was irreversible.

For a time, as we have already seen, beads assumed the same religious and social functions as earlier materials. Traditional dress, however, slowly lost its *raison d'être*. For practical reasons, schoolchildren, men who worked in town, and women, all adopted modern dress. This was of no great consequence if they did not remain outside the village for long periods. In such cases, Western garments represented only a temporary arrangement, enabling the wearer to pass unnoticed in town. In addition, in certain regions of East Africa, sometimes even to the present day, villagers were intolerant of those who continued to wear Western clothes once they had returned to the village. Wearing a Western outfit within the community suggested that one was denying its laws that dictated that each member must wear the dress appropriate to his or her sex, age and status, to give or obtain the respect that is vital to the proper functioning of the society. Thus, after a day or two, traditional dress, whether a draped piece of fabric, beads or red ochre, was readopted.

Although Western dress provided an acceptable degree of neutrality within an urban context, the option of changing back and forth between two forms of dress and thus between two worlds was not a viable solution. People had to take a stand, and faced with the pressing demands of modern life, any hesitation was of short duration. Ultimately, the adoption of Western dress represented the only way to obtain work and struggle against the foreign oppressor.

Furthermore, colonial enterprise contributed to the creation of a disastrous image for traditional dress, which became a relic of an obscure past, "primitive," and vaguely threatening to social stability. To wear such clothing equalled opposition to change, progress and development. Until quite recently, traditional attire was not valued but rather mocked and denigrated.

Figure 153 School cuts children off from education in their culture's traditional ways.
School in Maasailand.
Kenya, 1984.
Photo: Marie-Louise Labelle

Questions of modesty arose as well, and trousers and shirts for men, a dress or skirt and top for women, were universally imposed. Those who remained in their villages and continued to wear their traditional dress were ostracized. Schisms appeared between those who adopted the foreign way of life and those who continued to live in a traditional manner on a daily basis. In southern Africa, for example, the *amaqaba*, or "red people" who smeared their bodies and their clothing with red ochre were considered "heathens," as opposed to "educated people" or "Christians" who wore modern dress.

Early European explorers were the first to create a negative image of the inhabitants of eastern and southern Africa. Their fanciful descriptions of these peoples' physical appearance played a major role in helping Europe to legitimize its invasion of African territories and the subjugation of its peoples. Having established their domination in eastern and southern Africa, European colonists perpetuated this image in order to secure their position. Thanks to these images, Europeans soon created fictitious characters designed to satisfy their desire for the extraordinary and the exotic. Among these were the Zulus and the Maasai, to whom the clichéd "warrior" image has been applied for more than a century. Postcards showing "natives" in their "authentic" costumes were popular everywhere. To create such fictional personae, photographic sessions were organized in studios, and traditional costume was dressed up to make it more attractive to a European audience. The body delivered up to the viewer unveils a muscular masculine shoulder here, a young adolescent bosom there. Glass beads added an additional exotic note. In their time, these photographs had a political role aimed at minimizing the importance of traditional cultures by reducing traditional dress to a sort of carnival disguise.[1]

Beadwork played a primary role in this process. The first collectors of beadwork were unfamiliar with the social functions of the ornaments, which they regarded as "trinkets," or "curiosities." In fact, beadwork would soon become part of a commercial enterprise introduced by missionaries, included among the accomplishments of young African girls, as it was among those of European girls during the nineteenth century. At first, however, this craft enjoyed little success, partly because of the exorbitant price of the beads, but also because of a lack of interest among African women in making objects unrelated to traditional culture.

The increasing use of imported glass beads in ornaments thus coincides with dramatic events. It is everywhere a symbol of the colonial seizure of Africa's peoples, their lands and their traditions. For certain peoples, the short period during which beads became widely used marked the beginning of the end of their culture. It is only a few decades ago, for example, that the Dinka Bor of the southern Sudan adopted the fashion of beaded corsets and vests. A very short time after they had developed their current form, the entire Dinka population was persecuted, chased from its lands and reduced to exile by a murderous war. Consequently, during the 1990s, many beaded corsets could be found in galleries of African art and Western museums, probably bought from Dinka refugees in southern Sudan and northern Kenya camps. It seems that the beaded corset will forever be a reminder of the drama lived by the Dinka people and the emblem of a culture swept away by violence.

The San of Botswana began using a few glass beads in the early to mid-twentieth century. They developed a very personal aesthetic, one that bears witness to the loss of their former autonomy. When they started to use glass beads extensively, they were already confined to reservations and sometimes exhibited to foreign tourists. Having undergone forced settlement, they now make crafts in order to survive, using ostrich eggs from breeding farms.

Another striking and dramatic example is that of the Tonga of Zimbabwe. The flooding of their fertile lands in the late 1950s forced them to leave their homes and abandon all their traditional frames of reference. In rare photographs from this period, beadwork predominates, bringing a colourful and festive aspect to their appearance, contrasting sadly with the concurrent threat posed by the construction of the Kariba Dam. Similarly, over several decades and following numerous forced relocations, the Ndebele women of South Africa developed a unique design for their wall paintings and beadwork, just as their traditional culture was undergoing the final assaults of modern civilization.

The widespread use of glass beads in personal adornment thus represented both an unprecedented aesthetic evolution in the art of adornment and the decline of traditional cultures, combined with major upheavals resulting from an external threat.

In many cases, the fact that people reinforced the visual impact of their appearance through the extensive use of beads and bright colours, at the very moment that this external

Figure 154 Craftwork enables the settled San to survive. Botswana, 2003.

Photo: Paul Wellhauser, Nharo!

threat was being felt most keenly, was not a coincidence but a necessity. For many, the preservation of traditional dress worn on a daily basis (as is the case today for the Maasai) represented a way to resist to Western invasion.

However, the adoption of glass beads not only modified the wearer's appearance, but also changed the function of traditional adornments as part of a process that has taken several decades and is still not completed. The younger generations who still wear traditional dress have abandoned the heavy, massive and less-colourful ornaments of earlier times for lighter, more decorative objects. Women are playing a primary role in this process through the independence they have acquired in recent times with respect to their roles as wives and mothers. Samburu women, for example, who until recently still wore status ornaments, will voluntarily confide that these ornaments were "heavy," both literally and figuratively, and that they wanted to remove them.[2] Today, such ornaments are rarely displayed, except during important ceremonies when each participant's role in society has to be easily recognizable. These ornaments have not been suddenly abandoned. Instead, decade after decade, they have been slowly transformed in response to current fashions.

An example of this type of change can be seen in the formerly mandatory skin garments of married Maasai women. At the beginning of the twentieth century, women began replacing these garments with cotton fabrics draped around their bodies in the same fashion as the skins, i.e. fastened at the waist with a belt and knotted on one shoulder. Skin garments were still

Figure 155 At the time that the Kariba Dam was being built, Tonga women still wore their traditional beaded adornments on a daily basis. Kariba, 1956.

Photo: Darrel Plowes, AfriPix

produced throughout the twentieth century. Slowly but surely, however, women began wearing them only for ceremonies. By the beginning of the 1980s, they were sewing their fabrics lengthwise so that they closed along the length of the body. Finally, at the very end of the twentieth century, they adopted Western clothing such as dresses and skirts.

When used for traditional clothing, cotton fabrics pose a number of problems. First, the fabrics have to be purchased and then dyed with red ochre, which is also purchased. The ochre fades rapidly and the fabrics must be redyed and washed frequently, which necessitates great quantities of water, a luxury that most users do not have. Cotton also wears out much more quickly than skins, thus requiring frequent replacement. In addition, fabric decorated with beads is not sturdy; the weight of beads is poorly adapted to the cotton fabric support and the fabric tears easily. These factors no doubt precipitated the abandonment, for daily use, of traditional dress made from cotton.

Similarly, Zulu women adopted Western clothing very early but continued to wear their beaded ornaments as well, often on top of the new-style garments.[3] In many cases, notably in the semi-arid regions, repeated droughts decimated livestock herds and limited the availability of animal skins. In addition, famine forced women to look for other means of survival and traditional tasks no longer had a place in such a context. The adoption of Western clothing became a necessity rather than a choice.

The inclusion of glass beads in clothing and adornment also contributed to the abandonment of traditional dress: beads were expensive, and required the sale of precious goods. Glass

Figure 156 Maasai women dressed in cotton sheets. Kenya, 1985.
Photo: Marie-Louise Labelle

beads also broke more easily than metal, and since the fashions changed more rapidly with the constant adoption of new sizes and colours, it was necessary to replace them often. Where an ornament had once been made by gathering natural materials, using older beads inherited from grandparents, or bartering materials with neighbouring peoples, it was now composed entirely of commercial materials. The ornaments that had once been tokens of friendship or love passed from generation to generation became merchandise. With their new forms and colours, they lost their original significance along with all the emotional weight with which they had been endowed. Increasingly, people ceased to wear adornments that identified them or linked them to their ancestors. Instead they now wore simple decorations, which corresponded to the "jewellery" of Western societies.

As a result, many peoples of eastern and southern Africa look "over-decorated" between the middle and end of the twentieth century. Images of their attire are presented in coffee-table books that reinforce stereotypes about African people and ethnic differentiation.[4] It is primarily during ceremonies that all of the ornaments are worn. These ceremonies, which

Figure 157 This young woman is wearing a new version of the traditional Iraqw skirt in a cultural village. Tanzania, 1989.
Photo: Bilinda Straight

once marked the passage from one social status to another, and that were accompanied by dancing, singing, and the display of coloured clothing and ornaments, became a sought-after attraction for foreign visitors. An exotic image developed of certain eastern and southern African populations. In villages reconfigured as "cultural villages" — for example, Bomas of Kenya and Shakaland in South Africa – professionals replay traditional life, appearing to carry out the daily tasks of an earlier time. All are elaborately costumed in order to present the most exotic image for tourists. The reinterpretation of traditional ceremonies, turning important rites of passage into festivals in which regalia is one of the main attractions, has contributed to the folklorization of traditional dress and ornaments, the standardization of forms, colours and designs, and the disappearance of the original functions of these adornments.

Nevertheless, the women of eastern and southern Africa have gradually begun organizing themselves to take advantage of the tourist industry, primarily by making beaded ornaments for sale. At one time, beaded ornaments were purchased in the villages by intermediaries at very low cost, and subsequently sold at three times the price in shops in African cities, national parks and airports. As direct sale to passing tourists was no more lucrative, the women began forming cooperatives. In some cases, they also organized the various intermediate stages in their business, for example, renting public transport in order to travel to the "Maasai Market" in Nairobi where they could sell their beadwork. In southern Africa, where beadwork has long been a specialized activity, clients now fill out orders for the ornaments they want, based on specific designs.[5]

Ornaments destined for sale are quite distinct from those still worn on a daily basis. The clean, bright beads of the marketed product bear neither the fat nor the red ochre left by use, and their aesthetics are different. Their colour combinations do not necessarily obey the aesthetic rules of older adornments. Designs are more free-form as well, borrowing ideas from various sources. Many innovations are attempted. Elements and materials salvaged from urban life, including bottle caps, pieces of electric batteries, pens, plastic cables and pieces of rubber, are integrated into the design.

New styles of ornamentation have also made their appearance, often directly inspired by Western culture. The form of the beaded "watch" of the Maasai (*olkataar lesaa*), for example, was borrowed from real watches worn by Samburu and Maasai night watchmen. It has now become a common ornament within the entire Maasai community. The "tie-necklace" (*iqhina*) of the Xhosa is another example of a new style borrowed from Western culture.

There are very few small- or medium-sized objects that cannot be decorated with beads. They include modern items such as wooden utensils and key chains, and more traditional objects such as the wooden staves and fly whisks of village elders. Among the more typical products inundating the tourist beadwork markets from Nairobi to Johannesburg are dolls, beaded wire animals, beaded calabashes, baskets and beaded horns, coasters, beaded purses, hairpins and barrettes, brooches, earrings, necklaces and bracelets that can easily be worn by Westerners. In East Africa, there is a great variety of Maasai-inspired necklaces, pendants and bracelets, as well as beaded belts and leather sandals.

At the dawn of the twenty-first century, beadwork is also becoming more popular in the West. This is due, in particular, to the publication of several books and magazines dedicated to this art (not counting an impressive number of Internet sites), and to the huge success that this craft enjoys among girls and young women. As already noted, this was the case as well in the

Figure 158 Ornaments made for sale feature all kinds of aesthetic innovations.

Photo: © Canadian Museum of Civilization, Steven Darby, T2004-301

From left to right:

Necklace
Maasai, Kenya
2003
Glass beads, iron, synthetic thread
and animal skin
47.5 cm (l) x14.1 cm (w)
CMC-2004.54.5

Necklace
Maasai, Kenya
2003
Glass beads, iron, synthetic thread,
cowries and animal hide
107.5 cm (l) x 30.6 cm (w)
CMC-2004.54.6,

Necklace
Maasai, Kenya
2003
Glass beads, iron, plastic, plastic
buttons, synthetic thread and
aluminum
46.2 cm (l) x 14.5 cm (w)
CMC-2004.54.4

Olkataar
Bracelet
Maasai, Kenya
2003
Glass beads, plastic and iron
7 cm (h) x 8 cm (l) x 6 cm (d)
CMC-2004.54.2

Necklace
Maasai, Kenya
2003
Glass beads, iron, mirror, synthetic
thread, synthetic cloth and animal
hide
30.2 cm (l) x 21.4 cm (w)
CMC-2004.54.3

nineteenth century. Today, however, the context is radically different, as the contemporary vogue for beadwork in the West has a vaguely rebellious character. Ironically, beadworkers in the West are often inspired by African colours, patterns and techniques, as are Western fashion designers, who regularly feature beadwork and items inspired by traditional African dress in their shows for purely aesthetic reasons.[6]

At the end of the twentieth century, in conjunction with, or consequent to, the abandonment of traditional practices in Africa, there is a rebirth in the wearing of traditional beaded clothing and adornments.

In a modern context, traditional ornaments are no longer worn to indicate personal status within a society. Instead, they indicate an individual's association with a much larger group, often in opposition to the Western world. This group may be a particular people, but is more often a nation and, by extension, the entire African continent. The leaders in the wearing of traditional insignia are primarily politicians, for whom such a costume plays the role of emblem and rallying cry.

Figure 159 The first president of independent Kenya, Jomo Kenyatta, borrowed his name from his *kinyata* belt. Kenya. Photo: National Museums of Kenya

One of the best-known examples in East Africa is that of the first president of independent Kenya, Jomo Kenyatta, who not only wore a Maasai-style beaded belt on a regular basis, but also borrowed his public name from the name of the belt: *kinyata*, a term that once described a Kikuyu belt made of skin and cowries. Kenyatta began wearing this belt after a stay in Maasailand. Although it features a traditional beaded design (either Maasai or Kikuyu), it is a modern type of leather belt with a metal buckle, and must be worn with trousers. Certain Kenyans who live in an urban milieu or work in small rural towns wear this form of beaded ornament (another common type is the beaded bracelet) as a way of honouring their traditions in a discreet fashion. These belts are distinct from the belts worn on a daily basis in the countryside. They are neither tied to participation in ceremonies, nor do they indicate clear personal status as it is traditionally recognized. They have become a typical tourist product, and a very popular form of Kenyan beadwork because they can easily be incorporated into a Western outfit.

The message that Kenyatta conveyed to his fellow citizens by wearing this belt was twofold. First, it announced his separation from the West (end of colonialism) by displaying his traditional roots. In addition, it also opposed "tribalism" since this ornament was no longer of Kikuyu origin (Kenyatta's ethnic group), but a "composite" ornament that could be worn by

Kenyans of different origins. His goal in wearing this belt was to affirm national unity through a symbol drawing on tradition. Although some politicians, notably in Maasai territories, still continue today to manipulate certain elements of the traditional dress in order to attract the votes of the local population, the search for a "national" costume that would unify in a single image all the peoples of this country remains a very current preoccupation in Kenya. That such a costume has not appeared before now is probably due to the scorn directed toward traditional costume by colonizers for more than a century, as well as to the imposition of Western dress in an urban context. The goal of seamstresses and fashion designers in Nairobi, therefore, is to create a national costume using coloured fabrics enhanced with beads that will harmoniously integrate traditional elements to modern fashion. At the moment, Kenyans on official foreign visits continue to wear Western dress, while some borrow the traditional styles of other African countries.

Figure 160 Kakenya Ntaiya, of Maasai origin, studies in the United States. Here she wears a beaded bracelet in the image of the Kenyan flag.

Photo: Jahi Chikwendiu, *The Washington Post*

In South Africa, traditional dress has so long symbolized backwardness, largely due to its denigration by white missionaries, that it was long viewed with scorn among Africans who felt it did not reflect the values of a modern Africa. However, since the second half of the twentieth century, and coinciding with the rising importance of black liberation movements, traditional dress has reappeared as a way of reaffirming pride in African heritage. Beginning in the 1950s, Zulu kings in particular began to wear traditional emblems during major ceremonies. Such ceremonies (e.g. Shaka's Day and the Reed Ceremony) provide people with an occasion to express their ancestral heritage while coming together to affirm their common identity. During the ceremonies of the Nazareth Baptist Church, a syncretic church founded in 1910 by Isaiah Shembe, adepts don the costume corresponding to their age group, i.e. young woman, young man, mature man, mature woman, thus reviving and reinforcing ancestral roles in society.

As one of the objectives of this sect is to honour the ancestors, and since the wearing and the practice of beadwork is something of an obligation for women,[7] the traditional costume worn during ceremonies thus acquires an essentially religious function and by the same token, revives the former social function of costume as dictated by God. Considering that religious imperatives helped to precipitate its abandonment about a century ago, it is noteworthy that a religious congregation is playing an important role in the continued wearing of traditional costume in South Africa.

Another traditional costume that has endured to the present day is that of the traditional Zulu, Xhosa, Tsonga, Ndebele etc. diviners who wear garments and beadwork appropriate to their office. Once again, costume is enduring in a religious form.

Since the end of apartheid, traditional costume has been worn in a more obvious way on official occasions in order to re-establish a link with ancestors. As André Proctor and Sandra Klopper remark, "the wearing of beads has become, above all, a means of establishing and expressing a relationship with an independent African past. For this reason, modern beadwork draws heavily on the forms, skills, and symbolic power of the past, but has nothing to do with a return to any actual or particular past. On the contrary, wearing beadwork usually attests to the creation of new and … often conflicting and contradictory identities and social relationships."[8]

Figure 161 Mature woman of the Shembe church. KwaZulu-Natal, 2003.

Photo: Sibongile Nene, Research Assistant/Consultant for **Beads of Life** Zulu section

Uneasiness towards cultural differentiation through costume is the same in southern Africa as in eastern Africa, and attempts by some political figures to wear a costume that is very visibly attached to a particular ethnic group have been denounced.[9] The photograph[10] showing Nelson Mandela proudly wearing the attributes of a Thembu elder is misleading. In fact, except when he appeared in court in the early 1960s, Nelson Mandela always avoided wearing traditional clothing that might suggest his attachment to a particular ethnic group in South Africa, for fear of nullifying his message of national unity. As a result, his public outfit was usually characterized by the wearing of batik clothing or clothing imprinted with a common African motif rather than by costumes derived directly from the styles of his home region. In all of the contemporary practices relating to beadwork, from the revisited Xhosa costume, to Zulu-inspired beadwork mixed with modern clothing, and even the adoption of Maasai ornaments by South

Figure 162 Lorraine Klassen, singer-songwriter-composer, with one of her favourite necklaces. 2003.
Photo: Marie-Louise Labelle

Africans, the message is one of a pan-Africanism unifying all of the continent's peoples, religions, and beliefs. This unifying message is currently conveyed by artists including South African musicians and singers such as Canadian Lorraine Klaasen who mixes beads in styles as different as Xhosa, Zulu, Ndebele or Maasai in her stage clothes. However, she has also declared that on official occasions, she prefers to wear her Xhosa costume, albeit a modernized version.

A fashion show was part of celebrations called "10 Years of Freedom" held at the Canadian Museum of Civilization on April 29, 2004 to celebrate the tenth anniversary of the end of apartheid in South Africa. It featured examples of costumes that are now readily available to South Africans wishing to display their roots. Far removed from any notion of folklore, this event instead evoked a tradition that expresses a common desire for reclamation. At the same time, it is noteworthy that all of the elements of traditional costume presented at this event were "Westernized" in a way that universalized their aesthetic and made them more accessible to non-Africans. Once meaningful, such elements as the beaded Xhosa collar (that appeared on every costume but in different colours), the Zulu-style hat, and the drape of skirts and their button and beadwork embroideries have now become elements of a principally decorative nature.

During the latter part of the twentieth century, the beadwork of eastern and southern Africa gained the attention of collectors, no doubt because of its rapid disappearance from daily use. Certain pieces in particular were actively sought after, and were soon turning up in European and North American galleries. Museums organized exhibitions devoted to this art, notably in South Africa.[11] We are now having to come to terms, albeit much too late, with the lack of documentation on these objects long neglected by researchers. Discomfort vis-à-vis this little-known art form remains today, however. Beadwork has not yet found its true place among collections and exhibitions of African art, in part because of the uncertain regard in which it has been held for more than a century.

Although scholarly research in this art form is still in its infancy, sellers of beadwork aimed at the tourist market are never short of meanings to offer for beadwork colours and designs. Such explanations are the result of previously noted attempts by researchers to attribute meanings to the colours and forms of African beadwork. Each colour thus "symbolizes" an object, a quality or a feeling. An Internet site declares, for example, that "Black denotes sadness, loneliness or disappointment; but in a certain context black can also symbolize marriage or convey reassurance." This same site also boldly affirms that "the language of Zulu beads is deceptively simple. To interpret the love letter, one must know how to interpret both the geometric and colour symbolism … the three corners of the triangle represent the father, mother and child," and so on.[12] For several years as well, each ornament has been linked with a precise and stereotypical role in society such as "young girl," "mother" or "warrior," and is essentially described haphazardly.

The meanings offered to the buyer are thus little more than a sales pitch meant only to add value to the object. This sales pitch tends to accentuate ethnic categorization by cataloguing as "Zulu" or "Xhosa" beaded objects that are in reality of many origins, and feature standardized forms, colours and designs. Slowly but surely, the words describing provenance,

Figures 163 and 164 Xhosa- and Tsonga-inspired ensemble. Fashion show at the Canadian Museum of Civilization as part of "Ten Years of Freedom" celebrations in April 2004, marking the 10th anniversary of the end of apartheid. Designed by Ketso Mabusela and Angelina Ramaila.

Photo: © Canadian Museum of Civilization, Steven Darby

be it "Maasai," "Zulu" or even "Ndebele," have come to encompass all objects or exotic manifestations in a globalizing notion of the "authentically African." "Maasai beadwork," for example, has become a designation for all beaded objects from Kenya, even if they have never been touched by Maasai hands. Similarly, "Maasai dances" include all performances meant to display a showy exoticism to tourists. The word "Maasai" has thus come to describe everything recalling an exotic past that foreign visitors believe they can buy and for which they are eternally nostalgic.

Discussion of the supposed "symbolism" of the forms and colours of tourist objects has no merit because these objects are no longer used in context. Instead, such objects attest to the illusory nature of the relationship between buyer and vendor, in which the latter plays the role of both merchant and "informant," guide and intermediary, between a fabricated "mysterious" African tradition and a so-called Western "rationality." The buyers in turn seem prepared to be seduced by a marvellous tale that they half believe, and that provides the illusion of having encountered a hidden world. The creators of beadwork have themselves learned to create sales pitches based on colour symbolism. Many of them do not even wear these objects and are no longer aware of their original functions. The goal of the sales pitch is to infuse life into objects that have lost their emotional dimension.

This is undoubtedly one of the reasons why women of South Africa felt that it was much more important to create works in which narration had a place than to churn out necklaces and dolls for tourists. Thembi Mchunu was the first artist to produce "beaded sculptures" that

Figure 165 Tourism provides Maasai women with an opportunity to sell their beadwork. Kenya, 2003.
Photo: Kurt Kutay, courtesy of Wildland Adventures, Inc.

have since become very popular in South Africa. Made of a structure of iron wire or wood and stuffed with foam or fabric, they are heavily decorated with beads in very vibrant colours. They represent scenes from daily life, elements from the urban and rural worlds and mythological or religious scenes. Above all, however, they express the struggle of women against problems such as poverty or disease that they encounter in their daily lives. Some of these sculptures deal with dramatic and poignant subjects such as the death of children.[13]

Inspired to a certain extent by these beaded sculptures, women in South Africa along with women in other countries of southern and eastern Africa have begun mobilizing to create unique works dedicated to the struggle against AIDS. These works, which include basket weaving with telephone wire (*izimbenge*), are intended to raise awareness about AIDS and to raise funds, particularly in support of orphans. Several international exhibitions have been devoted to these works including **Break the Silence: Art and HIV/AIDS in South Africa** at the Fowler Museum of Cultural History in 2002. Organizations such as Siyazama, directed by Kate Wells and located in KwaZulu-Natal, play a leading role in the dissemination of these works on an international scale. Several of these works have an important narrative aspect, depicting orphans, mothers, crucifixes, dramatic representations of the scourge of AIDS as it is lived on a daily basis, or evocations of traditional mythology. Other beaded objects are created as well, including the famous red ribbon on a "Love Letter" that has traveled round the world. The latter incidentally bears two colours that have religious significance in South Africa

Figure 166 This sculpture represents children orphaned by AIDS.

Beaded Sculpture
Artist: Bonangani Ximba
South Africa
Cloth, plant fibre, glass beads and wood
45.5 cm (w) x 27 cm (h) x 8 cm (d)
Photo: © Canadian Museum of Civilization, CMC-2004.163.1, Steven Darby, T2004-302

and are used in particular by *sangomas*, undoubtedly not entirely by accident. Finally, there are beaded wall hangings, already popularized by Christina Nkuna and Given Makhubele, seen in Figure 169, that depict current events in South Africa and are now dedicated to the struggle against AIDS. In one of her beaded cloths, the artist Fokosile Ngema of KwaZulu-Natal (Figure 170) has established an analogy between a historical event experienced by the Zulu people and the current scourge of AIDS. The beads, like chalk-marks on a blackboard, create scenes mixing myth and reality with representations of figures, objects, elements from nature and written texts. There are few complex symbols to decipher. Instead, such works express cries of despair that must be clear and obvious to all. And although constant reference is made to elements of traditional life, ethnic particularities are not apparent in these works that are intended to reach the entire world and create global awareness of the problem of AIDS. Once again, although they are used as a simple coloured material, beads are still participating in the protection of individuals through the preventative information diffused by these works and the subsidies that their sale brings to women and children in need.

Figure 167 This doll represents a young Zulu bride concerned about the scourge of AIDS.

Makoti
Doll
Artist: Fokosile Ngema
South Africa
Cloth, glass beads, fibre, cardboard, iron, aluminum and wood
62.6 cm (h) x 18.3 cm (w) x 14.4 cm (d)
Photo: © Canadian Museum of Civilization, CMC-2003.199.1, Steven Darby, T2004-303

Some South African artists who use beads as a means of expression, and who are constantly reinventing the tradition of beadwork, also struggle against ethnic categorization. The artist Isaac Nkosinathi Khanyile is one of these. Of Zulu origin and a descendant of a family of diviners, he uses materials and forms from traditional art and mixes them with elements of modern life to create his works. Glass beads are one of the materials chosen, along with natural fibres, wood, clay, etc. Women make the beadwork that he uses on diverse forms[14] ranging from sculptures of the human form to traditional dolls, or even installations evoking altars erected to the ancestors. The beadwork is most often white with contrasting designs in red or black, the three colours used by diviners for their medicines. Unlike many artists who use beads as a simple material in their works, Nkosinathi Khanyile views beadwork as a tool for honouring the past and evoking the ancestors. Visions of his works appear to him in dreams.[15] Consequently, and remarkably, when set against current commercial creations, beads in these contemporary works have rediscovered their original role of protection, healing, and prayer to the ancestors and to God.

In his opinion, the motif of the triangle is a traditional symbol of healing in Zulu culture. In 2001, Khanyile said, "I am what I am, and I am what I was and ought to be. As an artist, I see myself as part of the community from which I come. It is my community that connects me with my past, my present and my future. Without this my existence would carry no

Figure 168 The Mother's Love AIDS organization in South Africa.
Photo: Khaya Ngwenya

Figure 169 The artist is establishing an analogy between the Zulus' bloody 1906 rebellion against colonial power and victims of AIDS.

Beaded Cloth
Artist: Fokosile Ngema
South Africa
Cloth, fibre and glass beads
126 cm (l) x 90 cm (w)

Photo: © Canadian Museum of Civilization, CMC-2004.163.2, Steven Darby, T2004-304

Figure 170 Artist Fokosile Ngema, 2004.
Photo: Siyazama Project

meaning. This is what gives me identity and feeds my soul, this is what allows me to realise myself as a being."[16]

This message that illustrates a symbolic return to their roots by many individuals from eastern and southern Africa is familiar to us. It brings us back to the reflections of some of the Canadians from eastern and southern Africa whom we met during the preparation of the **Beads of Life** exhibition. Many of them used traditional objects to evoke and recover a part of their identity. For some, these objects acted as talismans for remembering, for praying and for honouring their ancestors.

Figure 171 Traditional beadwork, costumes and utensils used in an Oromo marriage ceremony. Toronto, 1993.

Photo: Kuwee Kumsa, Research Assistant/Consultant for **Beads of Life**, Oromo culture

Kuwee Kumsa, of Oromo origin, attempted in Toronto to revive the tradition of the *siiqqee* woman's marriage stick and the *gorfa* milk container used in marriage ceremonies or birth rituals. When she came to meet us at the Canadian Museum of Civilization, she brought with her several traditional ornaments, including a simple necklace of white, red and black beads that has served as a sort of emblem for many Oromo in exile as well as those who have remained in Ethiopia. These three sacred colours, which had a precise meaning in traditional Oromo culture (see Chapter 4), were reinterpreted by new generations in order to evoke their recent tragic history. According to Kuwee, "White is the past, red is the present and black is the future … the past is symbolized by the white, because when people die, it is the bones and the teeth that remain, the skull … and when the fire goes out, what remains behind is the ashes … the red is the present because it is the blood circulating through the body, that's the blood that's being shed in the war … the flesh and blood, the black is the soul, it is the future, it is the unknown … it's dark but it is also the God, it's also peace, it's also purity, it's also holy, it is the future, it is the unknown, and that represents the soul."[17]

Included in the photographs she brought us was an invitation to her daughter's wedding in California. The invitation featured traditional Oromo emblems: wedding sticks, a milk container, ornaments of red, white and black beads, and finally, an outfit including the three Oromo colours, which are also the colours of their flag. For Kuwee, all of these objects were instruments by which she could "reclaim her identity" and continue to exist in Canada, her country of exile.

In the same way, wearing beads helped Njoki Wane,[18] a Canadian from Kenya, to recall the past, to connect with her ancestors, or simply to reassure herself and to gain strength. In her case the wearing of beads fulfills the same role as the burning of sage in remembrance of the ritual performed by her grandmother: "This is for reassurance, to have confidence in yourself."[19] Njoki was married to a Maasai and has carefully preserved her bridal costume. In her opinion, this traditional dress, which displays a particular status and a successful passage from one stage of life to another, was a source of power for women. Although she recognizes that she does not wish to live the life that they once led and still lead today, she would like to keep a part of that life with her in order to reconnect with a past that has either disappeared or is in the process of disappearing.[20] Her great admiration for and near veneration of women of the past is remarkable. Also noteworthy is her movement to bring together all Black women in Canada who have suffered some form of oppression, regardless of their origin. Her endeavour is original in that it consists of attributing a power that is at least political, if not almost sacred, to the beaded adornments and skin garments that once displayed what women accomplished as well as what they endured.

What is the difference between the possession of these objects by Njoki and the simple beaded souvenir brought back from Africa by a tourist? "Memory" Njoki replies, meaning the "memory" not only of an individual, but also of an entire people, the memory of its sufferings and its victories, as well as the need to preserve this knowledge for younger generations, both through these objects and through knowledge of the traditions they embody.

Some of these objects are still used on a daily basis. Tobacco, for example, enables Chipo Shambare, an intuitive healer of Shona origin who practices in Ottawa, to contact his ancestors in order to cure his patients' ills. There are also the white beads that Sibongile Nene wears in her hair to carry out her traditional work as a *sangoma* in Toronto. Similarly, in order to preserve their identity, Dinka refugees have made woollen corsets to wear when they dance during

Figure 172 Announcement of an Oromo wedding, California, 2002. Edossa and Huriya carrying modern versions of traditional wedding staffs. Huriya wears beads in the Oromo colours of white, red and black, and is holding a traditional milk container.

With the kind permission of Kuwee Kumsa

gatherings. The Dinka corset has thus become emblematic of their society, and a tragic reminder of a culture crushed by violence.

In conjunction with their commercial function, today's beaded ornaments also play an important commemorative role both in Africa and elsewhere. For many Africans of the East and the South, they have become emblems of traditional cultures that have either disappeared or are in the process of disappearing. Beaded ornaments also serve as a means of establishing a connection with a sometimes painful past as they evoke and honour the ancestors. Just as the distinctive emblems of different items of clothing and adornment have become uniform and standardized, the precise meanings that were once attached to adornments are slowly being erased. However, beaded ornaments are now becoming part of a much larger protest movement and an affirmation of a pan-African identity in which all traditional symbols can meet and mix, and in which individual preferences stem more from the vagaries of fashion than declarations of ethnic belonging. The message they send to the West is one of acceptance of the modern world, but a world in which history, near or far, is constantly recalled to memory with pride and veneration.

Endnotes

1. See the article by Virginia-Lee Webb, "Fact and Fiction: Nineteenth-Century Photographs of the Zulu," *African Arts*, vol. 25 (1) (Los Angeles: UCLA, 1992).
2. Labelle, 1985.
3. Interview with Sibongile Nene, Research Assistant/Consultant for **Beads of Life**, Zulu section, interviewed on December 10, 2003 in Toronto.
4. In books such as *Africa Adorned, The Maasai, African Ark*, and especially, *African Ceremonies*.
5. Information from Lorraine Klaasen, Research Assistant/Consultant for **Beads of Life**, South African section, interviewed on March 31, 2003 at the Canadian Museum of Civilization.
6. See, in particular, the interpretation of Dinka corsets by John Galliano.
7. Eleanor Preston-Whyte, *Speaking with Beads: Zulu Arts from Southern Africa* (New York: Thames and Hudson, 1994).
8. André Proctor, Sandra Klopper, "Through the Barrel of a Bead: The Personal and the Political in the Beadwork of the Eastern Cape," in *Ezakwantu: Beadwork from the Eastern Cape*, 1993, p. 57.
9. Ibid.
10. Guy Tillim, in *South East African Beadwork* by Michael Stevenson and Michael Graham-Stewart, 2000.
11. In particular, *Ezakwantu: Beadwork from the Eastern Cape*, South African National Gallery, 1993–1994; *Art and Ambiguity: Perspectives on the Brenthurst Collection of Southern African Art*, Johannesburg Art Gallery, 1991–1992; *Ten Years of Collecting* (1979–1989), Standard Bank Foundation Collection of African Art, University Art Galleries Collection, 1989, etc.
12. "The Story of Zulu Beads," The Beads Bugle, the Perpetual Bead Show. http://www.nfobase.com/html/the_story_of_zulu_beads.html
13. Eleanor Preston-Whyte, "Zulu Bead Sculptors," *African Arts*, vol. 24 (1) (Los Angeles: UCLA, 1991).
14. See in particular *The Trolley*, a shopping cart "dressed up" in palm fronds, woven grasses and beads, 1998.
15. See Rayda Becker, Rochelle Keene, *Art Routes: A Guide to South African Art Collections* (Johannesburg: Witwatersrand University Press, 2000), p. 125.
16. Virginia MacKenny in *Artthrob, Contemporary Art in South Africa*, 2001 (http://www.artthrob.co.za)

17. Kuwee Kumsa, Research Assistant/Consultant for **Beads of Life**, Oromo culture, interviewed on April 25, 2003 at the Canadian Museum of Civilization.

18. Assistant Professor in the Department of Sociology & Equity Studies, Ontario Institute for Studies in Education, University of Toronto, and author of "Back to the Drawing Board: African-Canadian Feminisms."

19. Njoki Wane, Research Assistant/Consultant for **Beads of Life**, interviewed on August 21, 2003 in Toronto.

20. "I do not want to go back to this life, but I do not mind having a piece of it, because by claiming, by possessing a piece of this, it connects me with some of the past, it can be a reminder of the oppression some of these women went through, of that whatever we are doing, we should not forget what happened in the past." Ibid.

CONCLUSION

At the dawn of the twenty-first century, beadwork is more widely practised than ever in eastern and southern Africa, although it is constantly evolving in form.

Throughout the twentieth century, women played a central role in perpetuating the use of traditional dress and ornaments. As we have seen, the materials used before the arrival of glass beads were meant to protect people and their possessions while also identifying their status. The colours of materials, such as plant fibres, red ochre, iron, cowries and ostrich eggs, later probably influenced the choice of bead colours. White, red, and black or dark blue had always played an important religious role. In forming contrasts of two or three of these colours, or with visually equivalent ones, women sought to make the protective power of beaded clothing and adornments as effective as possible. In addition, the choice of colours and contrasts, and the preference for certain shapes and their distribution in space, could evoke the configuration of certain social structures, although these analogies cannot easily be detected. These aesthetic principles applied to a very wide range of beaded ornaments, until at least the last half of the twentieth century, when the variety of colours, colour combinations and patterns exploded

Throughout the twentieth century, colour combinations were enriched, resulting in unparalleled aesthetic refinement. Geometrical designs grew ever more elaborate, necessitating complicated calculations on the part of the beadworkers. Figurative motifs appeared also, evoking familiar forms from the environment or sometimes, human figures. An explosion of colours and designs, as well as a management of space that grew ever more masterful, provoked many interpretations of the "symbolic" content of beadwork. Such interpretations tend to confine the wearers of beadwork and traditional dress to rigid and artificial social roles that reflect a vision of Africa that is, at the very least, oversimplified.

Whereas the roles of protection and status identification seen in older ornaments were maintained to a degree as beaded ornaments replaced them during the colonial period, the range of forms and colours used in beadwork and their meanings have multiplied over the course of the twentieth century. Only a few major aspects of ancestral dress still have a "stable" meaning, frequently amounting to little more than the silhouette of a person, defined by a traditional costume, whereas many of the beaded elements themselves have only a decorative role.

These changes in meaning are the direct result of the history of eastern and southern Africa over two centuries or more. Colonialism, conflicts, famines, forced relocations, poverty and development hastened the loss of traditional frames of reference in eastern and southern Africa, thus accelerating the disappearance of traditional costume from everyday dress. New circumstances have revived it today, albeit in other forms. The motivations that now encourage people to don traditional dress in public are very different from those of yesterday. Women in particular, wishing to free themselves from the masculine yoke, have slowly but surely abandoned certain "heavy" ornaments that displayed and reinforced their role as wife and mother in order to adopt Western dress or a "lighter" and more colourful version of traditional dress. This identifies them on a collective rather than an individual level, and reinforces their belonging as women. Signs of "submission" though they were, traditional feminine items of clothing and adornment have today virtually become "feminist" banners. At the same time, tentatively at first, then more and more visibly, many political figures have begun to wear certain telling symbols of traditional costume. Among men in particular, these symbols demonstrate the traditional qualities of the elders, such as wisdom and authority.

Depending on the period and on historical events at the local, regional and national levels, as well as the terms of the relationships maintained between the West and Africa, beadwork has undergone many changes of meaning and arrived at a crossroads. On the one hand, the extensive commercialization of beadwork has brought about a standardization of techniques, colour combinations and patterns. This in turn has led to a universalization of the aesthetic codes of beadwork, and the standardization of beaded objects that have gradually been "Westernized" to make them accessible to the greatest number of people.

On the other hand, this "universalization" is a sign of the desire among people of African origin who wear such beadwork to identify with an entity that is larger than the region and even the nation, namely, a pan-Africanism that encompasses people of all origins, languages and traditions. Slowly but surely, the wearing of beadwork has become a universal symbol of a collective resistance to Westernization, as well as an evocation of a past that is certainly long gone but continues to serve both as a support and a frame of reference.

Eastern and southern African beadwork has earned a new pride of place, not only among Africans, but also among Westerners who are including it more and more in their exhibitions and publications on African art. The role of women as producers and creators continues to be essential, and the names of beadwork artists are beginning to emerge.

The current rebirth of beadwork showcases certain aspects of traditions aimed at recognition of an individual or collective identity. Beadwork is still pervaded with profound political and emotional significance, just as it was when it was first made and used. These meanings are as various and complex as history itself: as this book is being written, a young Samburu initiate wears a necklace of blue beads to ensure God's protection; Sibongile Nene, a *sangoma* living in Toronto, wears white beads in her hair in order to communicate with her ancestors; some dignitaries attending celebrations in South Africa wear costumes inspired by the Xhosa tradition; and the boutique at the Johannesburg airport is overflowing with Ndebele-style dolls and beaded love letters bearing the red AIDS ribbon. Each of these uses of beadwork, taken at random, reflects only a small part of this continuing story.

Once ignored because of its obscure origins and even mistaken for a "mission" craft, the art of beadwork has never been as visible as a means of expression and affirmation of identity as it is today, both in Africa and elsewhere. As a talisman as well as a form of adornment, and above all as an open book on collective and individual African history, it is certain that it will still be practised for a long time to come.

SELECTED BIBLIOGRAPHY

Angas, George French. *The Kafirs Illustrated: A Facsimile Reprint of the Original 1849 Edition of Hand-Coloured Lithographs*. Cape Town: Balkema, Rotterdam, 1974.

Arnoldi, Mary Jo, and Christine Mullen Kreamer. *Crowning Achievements: African Arts of Dressing the Head*. Los Angeles: Fowler Museum of Cultural History, UCLA, 1995.

Art and Ambiguity: Perspectives on the Brenthurst Collection of Southern African Art (exhibition catalogue). Johannesburg: Johannesburg Art Gallery, 1991.

Barrett, Anthony J. *Turkana Iconography: Desert Nomads and Their Symbols*. Kijabe Printing Press, 1998.

Becker, Rayda, and Rochelle Keene. *Art Routes: A Guide to South African Art Collections*. Johannesburg: Witwatersrand University Press, 2000.

Beckwith, Carol, and Angela Fisher. *African Ark: People and Ancient Cultures of Ethiopia and the Horn of Africa*. New York: Harry N. Abrams, Inc., 1990.

Bedford, Emma, ed. *Ezakwantu: Beadwork from the Eastern Cape* (exhibition catalogue). Capetown: South African National Gallery, 1993.

Berglund, Axel-Ivar. *Zulu Thought-Patterns and Symbolism*. Indiana University Press, 1989 (first published in 1976).

Best, Günter. *Culture and Language of the Turkana, N.W. Kenya*. Heidelberg: Carl Winter, 1983.

——————. *Marakwet and Turkana: New Perspectives on the Material Culture of East African Societies*. Frankfurt: Museum für Völkerkunde, 1993.

Biebuyck, Daniel P., and Nelly Van den Abbeele. *The Power of Headdresses: A Cross-Cultural Study of Forms and Functions*. Brussels: Tendi, 1994.

Bigalke, Erich Heinrich. "Dress: Personal Decoration and Ornament Among the Ndlambe." *Annals of the Cape Provincial Museums* (Natural History). vol. 9,4 (1972): 65-90.

Boram-Hays, Carol S. "A History of Zulu Beadwork 1890-1997: Its Types, Forms and Functions." M.A. dissertation. Ohio State University, 2000.

Bourgois, Geert G., and Els De Palmenaer. *Legacies of Stone: Zimbabwe Past and Present*. 2 Vols. Tervuren: Royal Museum for Central Africa, 1997.

Brincard, Marie-Thérèse. *Beauty by Design: The Aesthetics of African Adornment*. New York: The African-American Institute, 1984.

Broster, Joan A. *Red Blanket Valley*. Johannesburg: Hugh Keartland Publishers, 1967.

Brottem, Bronwyn V., and Ann Lang. "Zulu Beadwork." *African Arts*. vol. 6,3 (1973). Los Angeles: UCLA.

Bryant, Rev. A.T. *Olden Times in Zululand and Natal*. London: Longmans, Green and Co., 1929.

——————. *The Zulu People: As They Were Before the White Man Came*. Pietermaritzburg: Shuter and Shooter, 1949.

Cameron, Elisabeth L. *Isn't S/He a Doll? Play and Ritual in African Sculpture*. Los Angeles: Fowler Museum of Cultural History, UCLA, 1996.

Cannizzo, Jeanne. *Into the Heart of Africa*. Toronto: Royal Ontario Museum, 1989.

Carey, Margret. *Beads and Beadwork of East and South Africa*. Shire Ethnography, U.K., 1986.

—————. *Beads and Beadwork of West and Central Africa*. Shire Publications, U.K., 1991.

Clabburn, Pamela. *Beadwork*. Shire Publications, 1994 (first published in 1980).

Colson, Elizabeth. *Social Organization of the Gwembe Tonga*. Manchester, U.K.: Manchester University Press, 1960.

—————. *The Social Consequences of Resettlement: The Impact of the Kariba Resettlement upon the Gwembe Tonga*. Institute for African Studies, University of Zambia. Manchester University Press, 1971.

Conner, Michael W., and Diane Pelrine. *The Geometric Vision: Arts of the Zulu*. West Lafayette, Indiana: Purdue University Galleries, 1983.

Conru, Kevin. *The Art of Southeast Africa from the Conru Collection*. Milan: 5 Continents, 2002.

Coote, Jeremy, and Anthony Shelton, eds. *Anthropology, Art, and Aesthetics*. Oxford: Clarendon Press, 1992.

Costello, Dawn. *Not Only for its Beauty: Beadwork and Its Cultural Significance Among the Xhosa-Speaking Peoples*. Pretoria: University of South Africa, 1990.

Courtney-Clarke, Margaret. *Ndebele: The Art of an African Tribe*. New York: Rizzoli, 1986.

Crabtree Caroline, and Pam Stallebrass. *Beadwork: A World Guide*. New York: Rizzoli, 2002.

Davison, P. "Some Nguni Crafts: The Use of Horn, Bone and Ivory." *Annals of the South African Museum*. vol. 70,2 (1976): 79-155.

Dell, Elizabeth. *Evocations of the Child: Fertility Figures of the Southern African Region*. Johannesburg: Johannesburg Art Gallery, Human & Rousseau, 1998.

Deng, Francis Mading. *The Dinka and their Songs*. Oxford: Clarendon Press, 1973.

—————. *The Dinka of the Sudan*. Prospect Heights: Waveland Press, 1984.

Dewey, William J. *Sleeping Beauties: The Jerome L. Joss Collection of African Headrests at UCLA*. Los Angeles: Fowler Museum of Cultural History, UCLA, 1993.

Diriye, Abdullahi Mohamed. *Culture and Customs of Somalia*. Westport, Connecticut: Greenwood Press, 2001.

Doke, C.M., et al. *English-Zulu / Zulu-English Dictionary*. Johannesburg: Witwatersrand University Press, 1990.

Dubin, Lois Sherr. *The History of Beads: From 30,000 B.C. to the Present*. New York: Harry N. Abrams, Inc., 1987.

Ellert, Henrik. *The Material Culture of Zimbabwe*. Zimbabwe: Longman's, 1984.

Fedders, Andrew, and Cynthia Salvadori. *Peoples and Cultures of Kenya*. Nairobi: Transafrica, 1980.

—————. *Turkana Pastoral Craftsmen*. Nairobi: Transafrica, 1977.

—————. *Maasai*. London: Collins, 1977.

Felix, Marc L. *Mwana Hiti: Life and Art of the Matrilineal Bantu of Tanzania*. Munich: Fred Jahn, 1990.

Fisher, Angela. *Africa Adorned*. London: Collins Harvill, 1987.

Galichet-Labelle, Marie-Louise. "Aesthetics and Colour among the Maasai and Samburu." *Kenya Past and Present*. Issue 20 (1988): 27–30. Kenya Museum Society. National Museums of Kenya (Nairobi).

—————. *Le Guerrier maasaï. Histoire d'un mythe, récit d'une rencontre*. Doctoral thesis. *École des Hautes Études en Sciences Sociales*, Paris, 1996.

Gardiner, Allen Francis. *Narrative of a Journey to the Zoolu Country in South Africa (undertaken in 1835)*. Cape Town: C. Struik Ltd, 1966 (facsimile of 1836 edition).

Grossert, John Watt. *Art Education & Zulu Crafts: (A critical review of the development of art and crafts education in Bantu schools in Natal with particular reference to the period 1948-1962)*. Pietermaritzburg: Shuter & Shooter Ltd., 1968.

Hammond-Tooke, David, and Anitra Nettleton, eds. *Catalogue: Ten Years of Collecting (1979-1989)*. Johannesburg: University of the Witwatersrand Art Galleries, 1989.

Hobley, C.W. *Ethnology of A-Kamba and other East African Tribes*. London: Frank Cass and Co. Ltd., 1910.

Hollis, A. Claude. *The Masai: Their Language and Folklore*. London: Clarendon Press, 1905.

Jacobson-Widding, A. *Red-White-Black as a Mode of Thought: A Study of Triadic Classification by Colours in the Ritual Symbolism and Cognitive Thought of the Peoples of the Lower Congo*. Uppsala: Almqvist & Wiksell, 1979.

Jolles, Frank. "Traditional Zulu Beadwork of the Msinga Area." *African Arts*. vol. 26,1 (1993). Los Angeles: UCLA.

—————. "Zulu Beadwork as a Record of Historical Events – Some Theoretical Considerations." Democratising Art and Art Historical History in South Africa: Proceedings of the 9th Annual Conference of South African Association of Art Historians. Durban: Technikon Natal, 1993, pp. 60–78.

—————. "Modern Zulu Dolls from Kwlatha: The Work of Mrs. Hluphekile (MaMchunu) Zuma and Her Circle of Friends." *African Arts*. vol. 27,2 (1994): 54–69. Los Angeles: UCLA.

—————. "Zulu Earplugs: A Study in Transformation." *African Arts*. vol. 30,2 (1997). Los Angeles: UCLA.

Joubert, Hélène, and Michel Valentin, eds. *Ubuntu : Arts et Cultures d'Afrique du Sud* (exhibition catalogue). *Musée national des Arts d'Afrique et d'Océanie : Réunion des musées nationaux*. Paris, 2002.

Kassam, Aneesa. "Traditional Ornament: Some General Observations." *Kenya Past and Present*. Issue 20 (1988): 11–16. Kenya Museum Society. National Museums of Kenya (Nairobi).

—————. "Iron and Beads: Male and Female Symbols of Creation. A Study of Ornament Among Booran Oromo," in Hooder, I., ed., *The Meaning of Things: Material Culture and Symbolic Expression*. London: Unwin Hyman, 1989, pp. 23–32.

————, and Gemetchu Megerssa. "Sticks, Self, and Society in Booran Oromo: A Symbolic Interpretation," in *African Material Culture*. Arnoldi, Mary Jo, Christraud M. Geary, and Kris L. Hardin, eds. Indiana University Press, 1996, pp. 145–66.

Kennedy, C.G. *The Art and Material Culture of the Zulu-Speaking Peoples*. Los Angeles: Museum of Cultural History, UCLA, 1979.

————. "Prestige Ornaments: The Use of Brass in the Zulu Kingdom." *African Arts*. vol. 24,3 (1991). Los Angeles: UCLA.

Klumpp, Donna. "Maasai Art and Society: Age and Sex, Time and Space, Cash and Cattle." Ph.D. dissertation. Columbia University, New York, 1987.

Korshel, Mohamud. *English-Somali / Somali-English Dictionary*. New Delhi: Star Publications, 1994.

Krige, Eileen Jensen. *Social System of the Zulus*. Pietermaritzburg: Shuter and Shooter, 1936.

Kumsa, Martha Kuwee. "The Siiqqee Institution of Oromo Women." *The Journal of Oromo Studies*. vol. 4,1-2 (July 1997).

Lambrecht, Frank L., and Dora J. "Leather and Beads in N'gamiland." *African Arts*. vol. 10,2 (1977). Los Angeles: UCLA.

Lambrecht, Ingo R. "Cultural Artifacts and the Oracular Trance States of the Sangoma in South Africa," in *Art and Oracle: African Art and Rituals of Divination*. New York: Metropolitan Museum of Art, 2002.

Levinsohn, Rhoda. *Art and Craft of Southern Africa*. Delta Books, 1984.

————. "Symbolic Significance of Traditional Zulu Beadwork." *Black Art*. vol. 3,4 (1979): 29–35.

Levy, D., and R. Keene. *The Horstmann Collection of Southern African Art* (exhibition catalogue). Johannesburg: Johannesburg Art Gallery, 1992.

Lienhardt, Godfrey R. *Divinity and Experience: The Religion of the Dinka*. Oxford: Clarendon Press, 1961.

Lindblom, Gerhard. *The Akamba in British East Africa: An Ethnological Monograph*. New York: Negro Universities Press, 1969 (1920 or. ed.).

Loughran, Katherine S., et al. *Somalia in Word and Image*. Washington, D.C.: Foundation for Cross Cultural Understanding, 1986.

Magor, Tomasin. *African Warriors: The Samburu*. New York: Harry N. Abrams, Inc., 1994.

Magubane, Peter, and Nelson Mandela (Foreword). *Vanishing Cultures of South Africa: Changing Customs in a Changing World*. New York, 1998.

Mayr, Franz. "The Zulu Kafirs of Natal." *Anthropos* 1 (1906): 453–71.

————. "The Zulu Kafirs of Natal: Clothing and Ornaments." *Anthropos* 2, 4-5 (1907): 633–45.

————. "Language of Colours Amongst the Zulus Expressed by their Beadwork Ornaments; and Some General Notes on their Personal Adornments and Clothing." *Annals of the Natal Government Museum*. 13,2 (1907): 159–66. Cape Town.

Mertens, Alice, and Joan Broster. *African Elegance*. Cape Town: Purnell, 1973.

————, and H.S. Schoeman. *The Zulu*. Cape Town: Purnell, 1975.

Mol, Fr. Frans. *Maa: A Dictionary of the Maasai Language and Folklore*. Nairobi: Marketing & Publishing, 1978.

Morris, Jean, and Eleanor Preston-Whyte. *Speaking with Beads: Zulu Arts from Southern Africa*. New York: Thames and Hudson, 1994.

Mthethwa, Bongani N. "Decoding Zulu Beadwork," in *Catching Winged Words: Oral Traditions and Education*. Sienaert E.R., and A.N. Bell, eds. Durban: University of Natal. Oral Documentation and Research Center, 1988, pp. 34–42.

Nebel, Arthur. *Dinka-English / English-Dinka Dictionary*. Bologna: Editrice Missionaria Italiana, 1979.

Nettleton, Anitra. "History and the Myth of Zulu Sculpture." *African Arts*. vol. 21,3 (1988). Los Angeles: UCLA.

————, and David Hammond-Tooke. *Art of Southern Africa: From Tradition to Township*. Johannesburg: 1989.

Pastoureau, Michel. *Blue: The History of a Color*. Princeton University Press, 2001. Originally published as *Bleu : Histoire d'une couleur*. Paris: Seuil, 2000.

Pavitt, Nigel. *Turkana: Kenya's Nomads of the Jade Sea*. London: The Harvill Press, 1997.

Phillips, Tom, ed. *Africa: The Art of a Continent*. New York: Prestel, 1995.

Plankensteiner, Barbara. *Austausch. Kunst aus dem südlichen Afrika um 1900*. Vienna: Museum für Völkerkunde, 1998.

Powell, Ivor, and Mark Lewis. *Ndebele: A People and Their Art*. London: New Holland Ltd., 1995.

Preston-Whyte, Eleanor. "Zulu Bead Sculptors." *African Arts*. vol. 24,1 (1991). Los Angeles: UCLA.

————. *Speaking with Beads: Zulu Arts from Southern Africa*. New York: Thames and Hudson, 1994.

Prussin, Labelle, ed. *African Nomadic Architecture: Space, Place and Gender*. Washington, D.C.: Smithsonian Institution Press & National Museum of African Art, 1995.

Reynolds, Barrie. *The Material Culture of the Peoples of the Gwembe Valley*. Kariba Studies, Vol. III. Manchester University Press, 1968.

Ryle, John, and Sarah Errington (Photographer). *Warriors of the White Nile: The Dinka*. Photos by Sarah Errington. *Peoples of the Wild*. Amsterdam: Time-Life Books, 1982.

Schoeman, H. S. "A Preliminary Report of Traditional Beadwork in the Mkhwanazi Area of the Mtunzini District, Zululand." *African Studies*. 27,2 (1968): 57-82; 27,3 (1968): 107-34.

Sciama, Lidia D., and Joanne B. Eicher, eds. *Beads and Bead Makers: Gender, Material Culture and Meaning*. Oxford: Berg, 1998.

Shaw, E.M. "Some Native Snuff-boxes in the South African Museum." *Annals of the South African Museum* (Cape Town), 24,3 (1935): 141-62, pls 24-31.

————. "Native Pipes and Smoking in South Africa." *Annals of the South African Museum* (Cape Town). 24 (1938): 277-302, pls 86-99.

————, and N.J. Van Warmelo. "The Material Culture of the Cape Nguni." *Annals of the South African Museum* (Cape Town). 58, 4 (1988): 447-949.

Sieber, Roy. *African Textiles and Decorative Art*. New York: The Museum of Modern Art, 1972.

—————. *African Furniture & Household Objects*. The American Federation of Arts. Indiana University Press, 1980.

Silverman, Raymond, ed. *Ethiopia: Traditions of Creativity*. Michigan State University Museum. University of Washington Press, 1999.

Sobania, Neal. *Art of Everyday Life in Ethiopia and Northern Kenya, from the collection of Neal W. Sobania*. Holland, Michigan: DePree Art Center & Gallery, Hope College, 1992.

Stevenson, Michael, and Michael Graham-Stewart. *South East African Beadwork, 1850-1910: From Adornment to Artifact to Art*. Fernwood Press, 2000.

Swantz, Marja-Liisa. *Ritual and Symbol in Transitional Zaramo Society with Special Reference to Women*. Studia Missionalia Upsaliensia XVI, Gleerup, 1970.

—————. *Blood, Milk, and Death: Body Symbols and the Power of Regeneration Among the Zaramo of Tanzania*. Wesport: Bergin & Garvey, 1995.

Tablino, Paolo. *The Gabra Camel Nomads of Northern Kenya*. Paulines Publications Africa, 1999.

Thornton, Robert J. *Space, Time and Culture among the Iraqw of Tanzania*. New York: Academic Press, 1980.

Thorpe, Jo. *It's Never too Early – A Personal Record of African Art and Craft in Kwazulu Natal 1960–1990*. University of Natal. Indicator Press Centre for Social and Development Studies, 1994.

————— and Eleanor Preston-Whyte. "Ways of Seeing, Ways of Buying: Images of Tourist Art and Culture Expression in Contemporary Beadwork," in Hammond-Tooke D. & A. Nettleton. *African Art in Southern Africa: From Tradition to Township*. Johannesburg: AD Donke, 1989.

Tornay, Serge, ed. *Voir et Nommer les Couleurs*. Nanterre, France: Laboratoire d'Ethnologie et de Sociologie Comparative, 1978.

Turner, Victor. *The Forest of Symbols: Aspects of Ndembu Ritual*. New York: Cornell University Press, 1967.

Twala, Regina. "Beads as Regulating the Social Life of the Zulu and Swazi." *African Studies*. Vol. 10:3, 1951.

Vanderhaeghe, Catherine. *Les bijoux d'Éthiopie : Les centres d'orfèvrerie de 1840 à la fin du XXème siècle*. Doctoral thesis in Archaeology and Art History. *Université catholique de Louvain, Faculté de Philosophie et Lettres, Institut Supérieur d'Archéologie et d'Histoire de l'Art*. December 2001.

Van der Jagt, Krijn. *Symbolic Structures in Turkana Religion*. Assen/Maastrict, Netherlands: Van Gurcum, 1989.

Van der Stappen, Xavier. *Aethiopia, Histoire, Populations, Croyances, Art et Artisanat*. Cultures et Communications, 1996.

—————. *Les Maasaï : pays, histoire, économie, environnement, croyances, culture matérielle*. Tournai: La Renaissance du Livre, 2002.

Van Wyk, Gary N. "Illuminated Signs: Style and Meaning in the Beadwork of the Xhosa- and Zulu-Speaking Peoples." *African Arts*. vol. 36,3 (2003). Los Angeles: UCLA.

Vogel, Catherine A. M. and Anitra C.E. Nettleton. "The Arts of Southern Africa." *African Arts*. vol. 18,3 (1985). Los Angeles: UCLA.

Wada, Shohei. "Female Initiation Rites of the Iraqw and the Gorowa." Africa 3, Senri Ethnological Studies. No.15. National Museum of Ethnology, Japan, 1984.

Webb, Virginia-Lee. "Fact and Fiction: Nineteenth-Century Photographs of the Zulu." *African Arts.* vol. 5,1 (1992). Los Angeles: UCLA.

Wembah-Rashid, J. A. R. *Introducing Tanzania through the National Museum.* Dar es Salaam: National Museum of Tanzania, 1974.

Wickler, Wolfgang and Uta Seibt. "Structural and Semantic Constituents of Mchunu Bead Language," in *Baessler-Archiv.* Beiträge zur Völkerkunde. vol. 39 (1991): 307-44. Berlin: Museums für Völkerkunde.

————. "Zulu Beadwork Messages: Chromographic Versus Alphabetic Notation," in *Baessler-Archiv.* Beiträge zur Völkerkunde. vol. 44 (1996): 23-75. Berlin: Museums für Völkerkunde.

————. "Color-Coded Zulu Bead-Language and a European Medieval Equivalent," in *Baessler-Archiv.* Beiträge zur Völkerkunde. vol. 42 (1994): 61-73. Berlin: Museums für Völkerkunde.

Winters, Yvonne. "Contemporary Traditionalist Bhaca and Khuze Beadwork from the Southern Natal/Kwazulu Areas." *Southern African Museums Association Bulletin.* 18,2 (1988): 47-51.

Wood, Marilee, et al. *Zulu Treasures of Kings & Commoners: A Celebration of the Material Culture of the Zulu People.* The Local History Museums, 1996.